The Complete Question and Answer Book on Dogs

Chris Walkowicz & Bonnie Wilcox, D.V.M.

The Complete Question and Answer Book on Dogs

Illustrated by Mary Jung
Foreword by Betty White
Introduction by Richard A. Wolters

E. P. DUTTON  NEW YORK

Published in the United States by E. P. Dutton,
a division of NAL Penguin Inc.,
2 Park Avenue, New York, N.Y. 10016.

Published simultaneously in Canada by
Fitzhenry and Whiteside,
Limited, Toronto.

Library of Congress Cataloging-in-Publication Data

Walkowicz, Chris.
The complete question and answer book on dogs.
Bibliography: p.
1. Dogs—Miscellanea.   I. Wilcox, Bonnie.
II. Title.
SF426.W35   1988   636.7   87-36399
ISBN 0-525-24664-9
ISBN 0-525-48387-X (pbk.)

Designed by Steven N. Stathakis

1 3 5 7 9 10 8 6 4 2

First Edition

To the Past: Justin, Caprice, Quinta, Calli, Brandy, Favour, Red, Kodi, Phydeaux, August, Opal, Otto, Trudy, Jet, Joey, and all the dogs we've known and loved
the Present: Marcy, Sally, Katie, Tigger, Bubbles, Henry
and the Future: whoever they may be.

C. W. and B. W.

Once I invited a dog into my house. Now my dog makes my house a home.

C. W.

Acknowledgments

We wish to extend our special thanks to Mary Jung, who pictures our every thought; to Ruth Wreschner, authors' representative extraordinaire; and to all the thousands of dogs who have supplied the answers to these questions.

We also wish to extend our gratitude to Betty White for the Foreword and to Richard Wolters for the Introduction. We appreciate the time they took from their busy schedules to add their thoughts, and their years of dedication to aiding and loving dogs.

Contents

PART THREE: **LIVING WITH YOUR DOG**

APPENDICES

Foreword

Dog found his way to Man's side about the time Man discovered fire. There he has remained through the ages, despite the countless times we remodel and modify him.

As the speed of modern life continues to accelerate, dogs not only manage to keep pace, but make increasingly important contributions to our well-being. They work for us; protect us; serve as our eyes or ears or extra hands; comfort our elderly; provide a conduit for our mentally disturbed. They dispel our loneliness, satisfy our need to be needed, and—they make us laugh!

My devotion to these creatures has been a rather open secret to the television-viewing public for more than a few years, and as a result, I am often confronted with dog-related questions—not all of them easy to answer. Imagine my gratitude at finding a book that not only anticipates those questions but addresses them in brief, clear terms generously laced with common sense and good humor.

The authors got to me from the time I read the dedication page, of course, but they kept me in their corner throughout. The answers are straightforward and practical, always keeping the dog's perspective in view. There is none of the high-flown rhetoric, so often encountered, that may sound great on the printed page but is a little hard to translate to your furry friend.

One of the most frequent inquiries I receive, usually couched in half-embarrassed language, is if someone should be considered weird because he *talks* to his dog. Personally, I have spent a lifetime including my pets in the conversation (and we all know there's nothing weird about me!). Dogs read our facial expressions and our body language so well—our tone of voice is simply one more means of communication. I was relieved to find Ms. Walkowicz and Dr. Wilcox of this same persuasion, encouraging verbal contact with your buddy at all times. Just remember he's reading your tone, not your words. You can help him know when you are playing and when you mean business.

Those of us lucky enough to share our lives with a dog must know that this relationship is a privilege not to be taken lightly. What we get out of it is in direct proportion to what we bring to it. Read on.

BETTY WHITE

Introduction

I have been asked to write an introduction to *The Complete Question and Answer Book on Dogs* by Chris Walkowicz and Bonnie Wilcox, D.V.M. I do not take this matter lightly.

The first objective I had to apply to this task was to question my role. Am I to introduce the authors or am I to introduce only the book itself? Struggling over this matter in bed last night, I concluded it was most likely my job to introduce *both* the writers and their work. I did recall, before sleep came, that I had discovered, while doing my own dog research for my Labrador Retriever book and my present research on the history of all the retrievers, that in the past *all* the great English and American dog writers used pseudonyms—false names to hide their identities. The famous Stonehenge was John H. Walsh; Idstone was Reverend Pearce; Frank Forster was Henry William Herbert; Dinks was Captain Peel; Richard A. Wolters is Richard A. Wolters, and the list goes on and on. But now, dear reader, I can assure you that Walkowicz and Wilcox are really Walkowicz and Wilcox. Then sleep came very hard, not because of the weighty problem I was thrashing about in the bedcovers but because Tar, my Labrador Retriever, who sleeps in his bed next to mine, snored.

Up early next morning to tackle the task, I was at the computer working this out by noon. Once I got all my facts assembled it seemed that an introduction of Walkowicz and Wilcox would be an easy matter. Hadn't I met them both the evening I was the after-dinner speaker at the 1986 Dog Writers Association of America's annual dinner and they were the recipients of the Book of the Year Award for their co-authored book *Successful Dog Breeding*? Also, didn't Mary Jung, the artist who is illustrating this book with over 60 delightful sketches, receive the Best Dog Artist of the Year Award from DWAA for her grand drawings in the breeding book?

As I thought further about this matter of writing the introduction, I concluded that there was little reason for me to introduce these two authors. They are already well known and respected. I'll bet my dog Tar's biscuits that dog people know these two authors. It might not sound very nice for me to say it about these two charming ladies, but W and W have been around the dog world a long time. Bonnie Wilcox has been a veterinarian for twenty years and has spent twenty-two years training and showing German Shorthair Pointers. She has published in *Dog Fancy*, where she has not only written articles but also a monthly column. *Pure-Bred Dogs/AKC Gazette*, *Kennel Review*, *Dog World*, and *Dogs in Canada* make an impressive list of magazines for which she has written. Also she has written *The Atlas of Dog Breeds*, with Chris Walkowicz.

Chris has been just as active, raising and showing German Shepherds since 1965 and Bearded Collies since 1977. She has had over twenty Champions and a fine book, a breed study of the Bearded Collie published in 1987. Chris has written over two hundred dog articles in all the important dog magazines in both the United States and Canada, besides six years as a dog columnist.

With credentials like these, I don't see any reason for an introduction on my part.

So I guess the important thing for me to cover in this introduction is the book itself. I read the manuscript from page one to the end and chuckled at the 63 drawings by Jung. There is an obvious sense of humor in the writing. You can tell that all three loved putting this book together. It's a bang-up job. *The Complete Question and Answer Book on Dogs* is just what it says. It's loaded with information and charming to read. Do you have a question? If you don't have one, think of one. Wilcox and Walkowicz have the answer. I tried my darndest to undo them, but every question I could think of about any phase of general dog information they had covered like the tent covers a dog show. Readers will be able to make wise purchases and be better and more responsible owners and could be spared some heartache. The authors have thought of everything from canine housebreaking to love. I counted well over 347 questions. I wouldn't know how to ask or answer that many questions about my children or grandchildren. Goodness, *are* there that many questions about kids?

When I designed my new home in Virginia, I insisted on one special feature—a telephone at the dining-room table. Hunters interested in dog training have for years been calling between the soup and the salad. Often they veer from the questions about the hunting field into general dog problems. Now, under the phone I'm going to put a copy of *The Complete Question and Answer Book on Dogs* by Walkowicz and Wilcox. Like the yellow pages, I want all the answers at my fingertips.

RICHARD A. WOLTERS

Preface:
Who Says You Can't Buy Love?

Perhaps John Foote said it best in his story "Allegheny."

> A man was paid to drop a . . . pup with a broken leg into the river in December to drown, but when he changed his mind and sought medical attention, the doctor asked why.
>   He replied, "He was so warm in the hand."
>   *Pure-Bred Dogs/American Kennel Gazette,* January 1981

It's easy to fall in love, especially when the object of your affection has big, warm eyes, floppy ears, and an appealing look that pleads with you to take her home. It's easy to fall in love, without thinking of the consequences.

Before succumbing to "puppy love," you should ask yourself some questions: Do you really want a dog? What breed is the best for you? Is this the right time of your life to have a pet?

An animal has specific needs: food, water, exercise, shelter, veterinary care—and love. If you cannot furnish all these, it isn't fair to you or the dog.

It's not a good idea to buy a pet for a child or a mate, unless you like animals too. You have to live with the dog also, and chances are you'll have to tend to his needs at times. Parents who grudgingly buy little Bobby a dog because "every boy needs one" will soon find fallacies in this argument. So will the parents of Jenny, who *promises* she will take care of the pup.

What about the electric train Bobby received last Christmas? Is he still spending as much time with it as he did the first month? Is the doll you gave Jenny for her birthday out in the sandbox minus clothing—or head?

If you bought the dog as a present for your husband, ask yourself who's going to watch the pup when your spouse goes on that fishing trip he's been planning. Chances are it'll be you.

And for someone who caved in to a wife's cooing about the cute puppy, don't forget the home schedule will change after her promotion. She'll be working longer hours, and you'll be walking Murgatroyd alone.

Should your spouse take a new job with extended traveling or your children not live up to their part of the bargain, you can't exchange the pup, return him, or cancel his subscription. That dog is going to be around for a number of years.

Your dog is "so warm in the hand." You can't put him in storage when you tire of him. It's unfair to dispose of a pet because you satisfied a whim with a spur-of-the-moment purchase. Thought beforehand will save later pain for all involved.

Some people have grown up with animals. Having a dog around the house is as much a part of their lives as a car, a career, or a friend. Circumstances may have changed in regard to living quarters, finances, and leisure time, however, and even lifelong dog lovers should keep these transitions in mind. Perhaps they can still enjoy having a pet, but current life-styles should be taken into account. Maybe a smaller breed should be considered—or an adult, rather than a pup.

Here is love money *can* buy. And dogs are expensive, even those given to you. The upkeep on a forty-pound, medium-sized dog will be nearly $200 per year. Dog licenses start at $5. If your dog is healthy all year, your veterinary bill still will be a minimum of $75 for basic exams, inoculations, and preventive measures. A good brand of dog food will run about $90 annually. Of course, a larger dog will eat more food.

Initially, you will also have the expense of collar, leash, bowls, grooming tools, pooper-scooper, chew toys, and housing. Later you may wish to fence your yard or enroll Duchess in training classes. Can you afford to supply your pet with these comforts?

After you've considered these matters and made your decision to join the millions of people who own dogs, you'll have questions of your own, which are answered in this book. Once you have all the answers . . . go ahead and fall in love!

C. W. /B. W.

PART ONE

BUYING YOUR DOG

1

The Love That Money Can Buy

When is a good time to buy a dog?

It's like falling in love—you know when it's right. If you want a stalwart companion who's never too busy to join you on a walk or to go fishing, who offers you his paw and a quick snuggle even if you have lost your job or flunked an exam, and who warms your cold feet on winter nights without complaints, you are ready to open your heart to a dog. And if you're willing to fill his needs, you'll be a duo "made in heaven."

Many new owners want to buy a pup in the summer. The weather is conducive to housebreaking, and children are home to help with chores and to lavish attention on the new pet. Dashing out the door ten times a day is definitely more appealing when it's warm and sunny than it is when it's twenty degrees below zero. Kids and pets are wonderful at entertaining each other (and using up some of that excess energy). But litters aren't always born at the most convenient season of the year, and a warm, snuggly pup makes up for chilly winter outings.

Where can I find this stalwart companion? How do I know what's good and what isn't?

Dogs are easy to find. But it is important to conduct some research, because it's worth extra effort to obtain the right dog.

Breeders who sell puppies and adult dogs advertise in the yellow pages, classified newspaper ads, dog magazines, veterinary offices, and show catalogues. A pet may be located through friends, in pet shops, in humane societies or pounds, through breeders at dog shows, through veterinarian or club recommendations, or on the street corner. Pet shops are able to display pups in public settings, and humane societies save lives; both are easily found. Although breeders are not as readily accessible, they frequently offer the bonuses of a home-raised environment with continual love and care, plus the opportunity to see the dam of the litter.

Prepare a list of questions to ask each breeder when you call. Ask your veterinarian or an experienced dog owner what you should look for. Most important, look for healthy, happy dogs. Run—don't walk—away from any that are scrawny, sickly, dirty, smelly, frightened, or flea-ridden.

Who gives breeder referrals?

First visit dog shows and study magazines or books to determine which breed you'd prefer. Then call your veterinarian or local club for recommendations. Write to the American Kennel Club (AKC), the United Kennel Club (UKC), or the Canadian Kennel Club (CKC) (see Helpful Addresses, p. 187) for the names and addresses of national organizations, and ask these for breeder referrals. Talk to satisfied owners, and phone other dog enthusiasts. Often a Boston Terrier owner is happy to recommend a friend who raises lovely Shih Tzus.

How do I find out who is a reliable breeder?

Call local dog clubs to ask whether they have referrals and whether they have an upcoming show, training session, or other event that you could attend to meet breeders and see their dogs. Ask a veterinarian for suggestions. No one knows better which people have the sturdiest, most stable-tempered animals. Ask friends who are happy with their dogs to recommend someone.

When you have a list, call to make appointments to see their dogs. When you phone, ask some of your questions. Don't wait until you are surrounded and besotted by bouncing, licking bundles of fur. Ask the seller whether she is a member of any dog clubs and how long she's been breeding dogs.

Does she train her dogs, and do any of them have titles? Ask whether you can see the papers and medical records; even if you don't know what you're looking at, they should be available. Positive answers to these questions are promising, although some conscientious breeders do not show or belong to clubs. While you're talking and struggling to remain objective, look for a rapport between the breeder and her dogs: a dog's head on her knee, a hand lovingly stroking a silken ear, a soft look of trust or twinkle of joy passing between owner and pets.

Should I buy a puppy or an older dog?

Most people want to start with a puppy, just as most hopeful parents want to adopt an infant. They want to enjoy and guide their little one through the first shaky steps. There is no such thing as an ugly pup, and new "parents" wish to cuddle and hold their bouncing bundle. Second-timers realize the joys of parenthood are tempered by puddles and nighttime yowls. An adult is often housebroken and trained in the niceties of doggie manners. It can stay by itself for a longer period and is through with teething. Moreover, what you see is what you get. No surprises.

Occasionally a dog becomes available when it does not turn out to be a sensational show winner, but it still can excel at winning hearts. Now and then an overflow causes a breeder to seek a good home for a retiree who is no longer able to be shown or bred. A kennel owner might feel Old Magic deserves to spend the rest of her life in the luxury of a one-dog home, receiving all the attention of doting owners rather than having to share the pats.

Should I buy a male or a female?

There are exceptions to every rule, and most of the beliefs involving male versus female can be followed by the phrase "but not always." Thus, females can be good watchdogs, and males can be loving. Not all males stray or fight with other dogs. Females are sometimes bigger than some males of the same breed. Although males don't have heat cycles, they are continually lusty. Neither male nor female urges are a bother if your pet is neutered. Environment and genetics have a greater effect on individual dogs than gender.

What about the all-American mongrel? My neighbor breeds Mal/Dals.

Mutts, mongrels, or mixed breeds are no more an American invention than the common cold. They're worldwide. With so many homeless dogs daily meeting a sad end, nothing is more irritating to dedicated breeders than misinformed owners who purposely or carelessly create mixed breeds. Facts show the mixed-breed dog has a smaller chance of obtaining a loving, permanent home than the purebred does.

No one would deny that many a canine of mixed parentage has found and given love to a family that swears it was the best dog they ever owned. Nevertheless, most buyers prefer a purebred dog about which they can foretell eventual size, appearance, and temperament. Unfortunately, this is unpredictable with an animal of uncertain heritage. There is no guarantee that a Malamute/Dalmatian mix will have a plush or short coat, erect or drop ears (or perhaps one up and one down), a sleek tail that curls over the back or a heavily furred one that hangs downward. Your pup may be spotted or plain. It could be white, gray, or a mixture. He may love pulling a sled or prefer trotting beside it. The mixed breed needs love too; just don't take any bets on how he'll mature.

Someone said I shouldn't get an inbred dog because that makes them crazy or sickly. Is that true?

Inbreeding suffers a bad reputation because of the human morals people use to judge animals. Dogs have no concept of cousin, grandfather, or even mother or sister. They are only following natural urges. Inbreeding doubles all genetic tendencies, the good as well as the bad. Depending on the luck of the draw and how the genes fall, a great number or very few identical genes can appear. Because dogs with severe problems should not be bred, no more mentally or physically unsound progeny should appear in a carefully planned inbred litter than in an unrelated one. Sometimes, of course, there is a recessive (unseen) tendency that comes through, which may occur in any type of breeding.

Knowledgeable breeders who study the backgrounds of their dogs often safely attempt inbreedings and linebreedings of high-quality animals—with good results. These experts must be certain they are doubling on good temperaments and healthy bodies. This is of the utmost importance in such a mating. A formerly hidden characteristic such as weak ears or missing teeth may surprise the breeder, but the pups should receive twice the genetic dose of sturdy bodies and sparkling personalities.

If you see an inbreeding on the pedigree, ask questions about congenital ailments. On your visit, observe the pups and parents for problems. If all seems well, you should have no fear of raising a four-legged psychopath or Quasimodo.

The breeder I went to wants to sell me a show puppy on a co-ownership. Is this a good idea?

Co-ownerships can be the start (or the end) of a beautiful friendship. Requests can be simple: co-ownership in name only (registering the dog with both buyer and seller as owners), stud rights, or a puppy from the first litter. The partnership can be a complicated web, however, with both people caught by broken promises and contract clauses requiring such elements as shared custody, hiring of handlers, and control of breedings. Sellers might also demand several puppies from all litters and a percentage of stud fees.

The purchaser may find co-ownership a way to obtain a better quality pup (that the breeder might otherwise keep) or to buy a top show prospect for a lesser price. The seller finds it advantageous to have somebody else pay the bills, yet still receives reflected glory if the pup becomes a star. This agreement also helps the seller retain a connection to his lines without filling another kennel, feeding another mouth, and doing more "pooper-scooping."

To prevent problems and misunderstandings, both parties should spell out on paper all demands and expectations in the beginning. If you intend to fulfill your part of the bargain and feel you can trust the other person, co-ownership can be a good choice.

I want to buy my fiancée a puppy for a gift. Isn't that a great idea?

Surprise gifts of animals are never wise unless you are positive the recipient would welcome one. The first time the pup leaves a *surprise!* on her floor, she may not find his winsome eyes quite so appealing. And when the puppy turns a designer dress into a teething rag, you may find your gift—and your ring—returned. Then you have an angry girlfriend, a homeless pup, a frustrated breeder, and a problem with no satisfactory solution. A dog is a living being and can't be shoved to the back of the closet if he doesn't "fit."

If you wish to surprise someone, first determine whether a dog is a desirable gift, then try to find out what kind: big, small; furry, sleek; active, laid back. Surprises are fun only if they're pleasant!

I want to buy my kids a dog for Christmas, but the breeder won't sell it to me then. Why?

Christmas is the merriest time of year—and the busiest. Parties abound, Grandma comes for a visit, everybody eats too much, and the kids become overtired from too much excitement. Add a puppy to the confusion, and everyone loses out.

The baby animal misses her homey-smelling blanket, her yummy food at the usual time, and warm littermates to curl next to. Instead she enters a strange place; is kept in the garage for long, cold hours; and is greeted with shrieks and grabbing little hands that poke and pull painfully. Little wonder that she crawls behind the davenport to escape or, conversely, becomes hyper—tearing off wrappings, chewing up Grandma's new slippers, tipping the tree, and running between Mom's feet—just as Mom carries the roast goose or Yule pudding into the dining room. All this hoopla stimulates the "leaky puppy syndrome."

As an alternative, give the kids mystery presents such as a dog-care book, feeding bowls, a leash, and a fancy collar. On a Christmas tree branch hang a photograph showing the pup decked in a red bow. A couple of gaily wrapped packages containing a chew toy and ball can be left under the tree to greet the new family member when she arrives a day or two later. The atmosphere will be calmer, and attention will be focused where it should be: on the pup.

I'm afraid of dogs, and Jeff, my future husband, has one. He's had Rufus for six years and refuses to give him up. So how do I exorcise this fear?

Acclimating yourself to dogs is probably easier than finding another husband or simpler than talking Jeff into giving away his pet. Start by asking yourself why you're afraid. Were you frightened by a dog as a child, or have you been bitten? Then remind yourself no two canines are alike, just as two people are not.

Start small. Play with a puppy or take a Papillon for a walk. Volunteer to brush your cousin's Welsh Terrier or to feed the next-door Flat-Coated Retriever while his family is on vacation. Consider borrowing a dog for a weekend. Work your way up in size until you're able to handle a Great Dane with aplomb.

Look for the positive things about Rufus. While observing from a point of safety, note the dog's reaction when Jeff returns from work—the wagging tail and the quick lick in response to the pat on the head. Watch their mutual happiness during a game of fetch. Offer to hold the leash while Jeff ties his shoelace. Before long you'll be wanting your own dog to walk!

I already have one dog, and I'd like another as a playmate for Chief. Should I buy another male? How about the same breed?

If your dog is as low-key and placid as Bob Newhart, any breed and either sex will fit into the household. If he comes on like Rambo—dominant and aggressive—find an easygoing pup. If Chief likes to think of himself as top dog, he will accept a female into his fold with more grace. The newcomer also should be large enough to escape injury if he's rolled over in a rough-and-tumble session.

Some breeds tend to be feisty with other dogs, and, if you think this is the cause of Chief's macho image, you may want to consider a type known for its peaceful tendencies. If you choose another breed of the opposite sex, you must be prepared to thwart any amorous inclinations. Neutering both dogs ensures that there will be no romantic relationships and helps create a calmer household.

Should I buy two the same age?

Having two pups the same age is like having twins. What one doesn't find for mischief, the other does. When one isn't puddling, the other one is. On the positive side, they keep each other company, and midnight moans are minimized. But the worst thing about having two dogs the same age is that they grow old together, and their loss is doubly poignant.

I've seen prices from "free" to several hundred dollars, and I've heard some dogs sell for thousands of dollars! Why do they vary so?

Like jewelry, dogs run from pretty dime-store trinkets to the Hope diamond. "Hope" is apropos to purchase prices in the thousands. The buyer hopes the dog will look classy and live up to its reputation.

Prices vary according to abilities, pedigree, titles, show potential, breeder's reputation, age of the dog, local economy, rarity of the breed, and the expense in breeding and raising the litter.

What is "pick" of the litter? How can I be sure I'm getting the pick?

Like the versions of three witnesses, "pick" can be different, depending on individual preference. For the single woman living in a high-crime district, this can mean the pup who alerts at every sound. The young couple expecting a baby may choose the happy-go-lucky pup who's friendly yet able to take his lumps. The breeder may select one that reminds her of a favorite dog, and a show enthusiast will leave with the one that has outstanding movement and type. A "pick" puppy can be the first chosen, or it can be the last if it's the right dog for you.

If you are concerned about having first choice, you must specify that to the breeder when you make a deposit, and you must be prepared to pay dearly for that privilege. Remember, the "pick" of a poor litter may not compare favorably with the "leftover" in a superior litter.

How do I choose one out of a whole litter?

New buyers often are adamant about a particular sex, color, or type. Experienced owners occasionally want one "just like old Betsy." The best characteristic to seek is a suitable personality. If you buy the pup for color or size, you may find yourself with a dog who drives you nuts: he barks too much; she's afraid of her shadow. And even if you discover Sweet Betsy's clone, her mirror image may behave more like a grizzly than Betsy.

Ask yourself questions: Do you want a dog that lies beside your rocker or one that jogs five miles with you daily? Do you want a dog to train in obedience? Then pick the pup that's alert and biddable. If you want to show, you should seek the charismatic pup, one with the look-at-me strut, as well as one that has good show points. No matter how attractive, if the pup doesn't sparkle, it won't be a top winner.

If you've found a breeder you trust, ask her opinion. She's watched the puppies for weeks, noting which is quiet, which is bouncy, and which is willing to please. Tell her what you want in a pup and ask her to help you choose.

What is the best age to take my puppy home?

Studies have shown puppies need to nurse from their mother until about five weeks old and need the companionship of their littermates until about seven to eight weeks. When a pup is eight to ten weeks, it's an ideal time to bring him home. At that age, the dog should have had a veterinary exam, received his first preventive inoculations, and been wormed if necessary. It should be weaned to puppy food and ready to begin housebreaking and walking on leash.

What about a pound pup or stray dog? Do I dare give my heart to a dog somebody else dumped?

When background is uncertain, a dog may be hazardous to your happiness and pocketbook. Try to determine why the animal was discarded. Was he a barker, a biter, or gun-shy? Nevertheless, if you give your heart and your home to a stray, whether purebred or mongrel, you are performing a good deed. It is ideal for the dog, because the ultimate end for many of these castoffs is death. It's also good for society because this particular dog will not bite and run, dirty the streets, strew garbage, or chase and destroy farm stock.

Sometimes the reason for the discarding is no fault of these dogs. They need homes too and, just as kids with an abused or neglected past grow up to justify their foster parents' faith, many of these dogs warm owners' hearts and hearths.

Be prepared for surprises. Pounds are not always discerning of the genetic makeup of the dog, and many a five-week-old "terrier mix" has grown to a ninety-pound behemoth by eight months.

Why do books stress "look at the mother"?

Since the father is usually just a "one-night stand," or at best a two-day fling, he's often "out of town" or in the midst of a permanent separation by the time the results of his escapade are visible. The best he can hope for is visitation. The mother not only passes her genotype to her babes, as does the sire, but she influences them through environmental conditioning. If Mom's nervous and jumpy, you can bet her pups will be too. Grumpy mothers often put chips on their kids' shoulders too. But if she's alert, friendly, calm, and playful, or exhibits any of the characteristics you want in your dog, it's likely these traits will rub off on her little ones.

Will my puppy grow up looking like the parents?

As much as your kids look like you—maybe. Or maybe she'll look like Great-aunt Flopsy, and he'll look like Grandpa Megabucks. There will be some similarities, of course, and once in a while a pup is born that is the mirror image of a parent. The greatest influence comes from the sire and dam, with correspondingly less from the grandparents and the great-grandparents. After three generations, the percentage of inheritance is so small as to be minimal, and the influence of a Champion or two out of 126 ancestors is well diluted. Every now and then, however, Mother Nature plays a trick; and the infant looks just like Great-great-great-uncle Harry, the horse thief, or Great-great-great-uncle Hairy, the egg-suckin' dawg.

What is the difference between a show dog and a pet?

A show dog is often a pet, but a pet is not always showable, just as a rose is a flower, but a flower is not always a rose. A fine line exists between what makes a show "flyer" and what labels a pet or companion, something as ephemeral as attitude, or as substantial as ears that should stand but won't (or do stand and shouldn't!).

Show prospects are considered to have the best chance of finishing their Championships—no major faults, a designer form, that certain sparkle, a gait that takes the connoisseur's breath away. These dogs wear breathtaking price tags too. Even among show pups, the quality can be variable. Anything is possible, from the dog that a judge forgets as it leaves the ring, to the one who makes her say *Wow!*, or the one that she offers to buy at any price.

The pet is not necessarily inferior or defective, any more than we are when we don't become president or Miss World. A pet has the important parts such as a tail for wagging, a tongue for kissing, and four legs all in the right corners. He may be a bit big or, conversely, too small, a characteristic that may actually be preferable to his buyer. Coat color may be "off," in the wrong places, too much or too little. Teeth may be missing or crooked, and the coat may be less than ideal. In males, one or both testicles may be undescended. But, after all, who cares about color, size, or hair when you're looking for a friend?

If you've uncovered an outstanding litter owned by a conscientious breeder, the one termed pet in his litter could actually be better than the "pick" of another.

Brandy is getting really old. Would it be OK to buy another dog now?

If you believe your gray-haired gal can adjust to the rousing romp-ishness of a pup, you won't have to face the inconceivable task of replacing a friend. Some old-timers welcome a youngster; the pup's energy and sheer joy of being alive give the senior citizen a nudge, jolting her back into the world of puddles, shared toys, and ears used for teething. If Brandy is in good health, enjoys the company of other dogs, and is not too set in her ways, a pup can give her a new "leash" on life. It can give her a lilt to her step, a renewed gleam to her eye. Some begin playing games again, doing things they haven't found interesting in years. This stimulation sometimes aids your old-timer to live longer and to enjoy life more.

Base this decision on your older dog and, if you decide to add another, adjust the pup's schedule to Brandy's. Never forget Brandy was your friend first and should enjoy certain privileges. Too soon the pup will have his turn at your undivided attention.

I've got a chance to get a super dog for nothing. Isn't that wonderful?

The freebie is not always free. Necessary shots, worming, high-quality food, and veterinary care are rare to nonexistent when a new litter is offered to takers at no cost.

Ask yourself why you are the lucky recipient of Super Dog. Is it because he has been a juvenile delinquent? Does he bark day and night? If there are no problems, why is he being given away? If he were such a wonder, wouldn't his present owners want to keep him or wouldn't he have been snatched up for "best offer"? Of course, sometimes owners find their circumstances changed by a move, a divorce, or a job loss, and their main concern is to find their pet a good home. Other times, it's because they have tried to place him and had no luck.

Whether a puppy or an adult, a dog usually is valued more when it's been bought, like other belongings. Too often, owners tend to be careless of that which comes too easily. The "Oh, well, if Lulu is run over, we'll just get another" feeling often prevails. It's easy come, easy go.

If both the dog and your attitude are healthy, however, then there is no reason to look your gift dog in the mouth.

My dog just died. Should I buy a new one right away?

The decision of one grieving master may be never to own or give his heart to another animal. He can't face the heartbreak. Some people don't believe their house is a home without a pet and buy another immediately. Yet others allow time to ease the pain and to select their new companion wisely.

Don't try to replace your last dog; you can't do it, any more than you can replace a friend. There will never be another set of eyes so brown, or another dog so clever she knows what you're going to do before you do yourself. You may consider another breed, the opposite sex, or another color. Even if you found a dog that looked just like ol' Misty or even kept one of her pups, it's unlikely the new one would behave in the same way.

Never make the mistake of comparing the new pet with her predecessor. It's unfair to the newcomer, as the deceased is often elevated to the level of saint. If Moppet puddles on the floor, you'll forget the accidents Misty had ten years ago. The teeth marks on the chair leg have been there so long nobody can remember whether it was Misty or your baby who did it. The nose prints on the window haven't been there since Misty stopped caring who walked past the house. And the well-worn dent in the sofa cushion is all the dearer because it was hers.

You can't expect lively, precocious, svelte Moppet to act as if she were overweight, shuffling, nearsighted Misty. Dogs are not machines. They don't make photocopies.

I'm going to buy a puppy soon. What will I need before I get him?

It's a good idea to wait for most purchases until you've talked to the breeder. But you may want to obtain a nylon or leather puppy leash and collar. (Chain leashes wreak havoc on hands when a dog pulls on the leash.) A chew toy or two and bowls for food and water complete the shopping list until you can learn what kind of food and grooming equipment you will need.

Should I look at more than one litter?

You may not always have an opportunity to look at more than one litter of Chinooks or Xoloitzcuintlis, but comparison shopping may be advantageous. Even looking at two litters of different breeds can give you an idea of personality and quality. Talking to one breeder can suggest questions to ask another. For instance, if one Saint Bernard owner boasts his dogs are all certified for good hips, you should ask the second breeder whether the sire and dam of *her* litter are x-rayed clear. If one breeder's prices are much higher than another's, try to find out why—does he offer a health guarantee, Champion parents, and a rebate on obedience titles? If so, are those things worth one hundred dollars more to you? Looking at more than one litter allows you to weigh the advantages of each. As when buying peanut butter, it pays to be choosy.

What do I say when I'm talking to someone on the phone, and I'm not sure? What should I say if I don't like the dog when I see him? I hate hurting someone's feelings.

If you receive "bad vibes" or don't like the pup, tell the seller you're going to look at other litters before you make up your mind. Don't take a dog home because you feel sorry for it, or you may feel sorry for the next ten or more years.

Don't make false promises: "I'll call you again on Sunday." "I'll be back with my husband tomorrow." "Give me the directions, and I'll be there in half an hour."

Be prompt for your appointment. Breeders have busy lives and may have plans after your visit. They may have postponed departure for a show to meet you, or stayed home from a club meeting to wait for your call. They may have six dogs to groom, a mating to handle, and another prospect whom they are holding off for you. Many of them have families and nondoggy activities as well. If you find you cannot make your appointment, call to change or cancel it. It's upsetting for breeders to bathe four pups and have no one show up at the party!

The dog I'm going to look at was "returned to the breeder." Does that mean there's something wrong with him?

Not necessarily. Second marriages are often happy ones. Sometimes pups sold as show prospects don't make the grade; that elusive quality is just missing. He's not a showman, or she went oversize. Occasionally, it's not the pup at all, but the buyer's personal circumstances that cause the return, such as a move to a condo, loss of income, or the animosity of a "first" dog toward the newcomer. Try to find out why this dog was returned. Is it a defective model, or did it just not fit?

How do I find out whether health problems exist in the breed? How can I know whether their dogs are free of these problems?

Read, study, and ask questions; talk to a veterinarian. Make yourself as aware as possible of breed predispositions. Listings of these are found in *Successful Dog Breeding* by Chris Walkowicz and Bonnie Wilcox, D.V.M., and in *Medical and Genetic Aspects of Purebred Dogs* by Ross Clark, D.V.M., and Joan Stainer. If you are concerned about various diseases or deformities such as hip dysplasia, juvenile cataracts, or von Willebrand's disease, ask whether the parents have been certified free of the problem.

That's why it's so important to find a reliable breeder. His reputation depends on satisfied customers, time after time. The quick-buck schemer or unknowledgeable one-time seller doesn't care whether you refer your brother-in-law next year.

Try to ascertain whether the seller is concerned about soundness.

Does he breed for the sturdiest possible dog? Be suspicious of the person who states categorically, "I have no problems." No dog—purebred or mixed—is perfect, just as we, their owners, are not. The breeder who discusses temperament or hereditary faults and then tells you how he is trying to avoid them is preferable to those who take the ostrich approach and bury their heads in the sand.

2

The Match Game

How many breeds of dogs do I have to choose from? What types of dogs are there?

Cynologists have unearthed more than 400 breeds currently in existence. In North America alone, 152 are recognized by major canine registries in the United States and Canada.

The American Kennel Club (AKC) classifies breeds into seven groups: Sporting, Hound, Working, Terrier, Toy, Non-Sporting, and Herding. Dog experts have divided the breeds according to use, type, or origin such as flock guarding, mastiff, hound, gun dog, northern, herding, terrier, and southern. In this manner of classification, the miniatures and Toys are placed in their respective groups along with their larger counterparts.

I'll never be able to choose! How do I decide which breed?

Pair off the various breeds in your mind (or on paper) and pick your winner—big versus small, long hair versus short, active versus lethargic, noisy versus quiet, rare versus common, protective versus peaceful. Which suits your aesthetic taste, a Mastiff, Afghan, Giant

Schnauzer, or Bichon Frise? What type do you find more appealing? Before long you'll have the winners of your mental competitions narrowed down to three or four. When you find breeds that attract you, make certain that their personalities fit your expectations. Don't buy a Brittany and be upset when he doesn't guard your home or be disappointed when your Chow doesn't effusively greet your visitors.

Price and availability can assist you to make a final choice. No matter what your preference, study the mother. Could you live with her?

Give yourself sufficient time to search for your future companion and be a little flexible, willing to give a bit on a point or two. You can't always find a fawn, pet-quality female Bearded Collie within twenty-five miles for Father's Day, especially if you don't start looking until June 1 and you've set a $100 limit.

Where do I find information on my particular choice of breed?

Write to the kennel clubs and ask for the addresses of breed-specialty clubs. Many have free informational brochures and publications to which you can subscribe. All-breed magazines such as *Pure-Bred Dogs/American Kennel Gazette*, *Bloodlines*, *Dogs in Canada*, *Dogs USA*, *Dog Fancy*, *Dog World*, and *Kennel Review* feature a breed or two each issue, along with advertisements for dogs. In addition, books give in-depth information on one or more breeds. Clubs, breeders, bookstore clerks, and librarians all can provide you with suggestions. Addresses for these magazines are listed under Helpful Addresses, page 187.

I've heard certain breeds are "one-person" or "one-family" dogs. Is this true?

Most dogs prefer their own families to strangers, although now and then you find a dog that is a four-legged Will Rogers, who never met a man he didn't like. Several breeds are aloof to outsiders and tolerate, but don't invite, attention from anyone other than their owners. Not all of these are protective breeds; some are just not party animals. Some individuals are even more prickly about being touched, making these canine porcupines difficult for the average family to live with.

What breeds make good watchdogs?

Although certain breeds were developed for protection—Kuvasz, Rottweiler, and Doberman Pinscher, for instance—any dog that barks will suit the purpose. Your choice is not limited to large dogs, however, as a bite in the ankle can hurt just as much as one in the posterior. Police statistics show that intruders usually pass by the house from which yaps, growls, snarls, and other alarm sounds are emitted and go next door, where there is no "music" to burgle by. This means a Poodle or Yorkshire Terrier can be as good an alarm dog as a Great Dane.

Dogs that are devoted to their owners are more likely to be protective if put to the test. Some dogs, however, are just so agreeable they greet the burglar at the door and show him the silver. Others may be so aggressive that they must be put into another room before anyone is allowed into the house. Watchdogs do no good if they must be confined every time anyone treads on your property.

What breeds are good with kids? Is there a breed that they can easily handle?

Kids and dogs go together like peanut butter and jelly, spring and baseball, and clowns and the circus. Some breeds believe children were made for them. Put a Golden Retriever, Collie, or Newfoundland with a youngster, and the dog will think he's in heaven.

Most breeders advise choosing a dog that is large enough to cope with normal childhood rowdiness. Many sporting, herding, and working breeds are notoriously gentle with children and can all survive a toddler's fall on them or tolerate an infant's teething on their ears. When one of these beasties grows weary of little Sarah's dressing him as her baby doll, or of Melvin's using him as a tackling dummy for football practice, he simply leaves. No fuss, no fight. The worst that happens is that the infant can be knocked over on her well-padded bottom. Sometimes the only defense a little dog has is his teeth. Some Toys do fine with youngsters; however, it depends on the dog—and the children.

Just remember not every dog appreciates the finer qualities of children: screeching, running, jumping, slamming doors, or strange kids yelling and waving their arms. Look for a dog with patience and a natural affection for children.

Is it true mongrels are smarter and healthier?

People who are half-German and half-Swedish are no more healthy or intelligent than those who are pure German or Swedish. The old theory was that mixed breeds had to be smarter and healthier to survive. That's not necessarily true; they may just be luckier.

As in all genetics, the progeny can inherit only what the parents have to give. Breeders of purebred dogs, however, can study pedigrees and then breed into lines that have demonstrated intelligence. Responsible breeders plan all matings with sound parents.

Since miscegenation, or "mixed marriage," is unplanned except by the two protagonists, it is difficult to predict the results. If the father is an Obedience Trial Champion Bernese and the mother a sturdy Field Trial Champion Weimaraner, new owners are in luck. The pups may receive brains and vigor from both. But if the sire is an idiot and the mother lame, the offspring may be little Frankensteins. If the sire is a traveler who wooed, won, and lost his ladylove in an hour, you can't be sure whether he's smart, stupid, robust, or a raving maniac.

If you fall in love with a "Heinz 57," so be it. Many mixed breeds are delightful companions, but be sure you pick your little mix because of his own appeal, not because of old wives' tales.

I'm afraid of big dogs, and that's what my husband wants. Aren't they all mean?

You can't judge a breed by its cover or its reputation. Exceptions are the rule: sweet, loving German Shepherds and Rottweilers abound, and nasty-tempered Pomeranians or Shih Tzus can be found. Each dog should be judged on his own merits. Fallacies such as "All Dobes are mean" and "All Pit Bulls are killers" are as untrue as "All redheads have terrible tempers" and "All blondes have more fun."

Do your homework. Select a docile, affable pup from docile, affable parents. In other words, pay attention to his tail, rather than his tale.

I want a breed that will be a lapdog, or at least lie next to me in my recliner. Which breeds will do that?

All! Some just fit better than others.

I prefer a placid animal. Which breeds are the most quiet and sedate?

You've just eliminated the majority of Terriers, Sporting, Hound, and Herding breeds, and several others, all of whom require regular exercise and outings. You may want to consider a Bulldog or a Basset Hound, both less active breeds, whose favorite activity often is sniffing the kitchen floor after meals and sinking with a sigh at your feet.

There's a difference between being inactive, however, and simply not being a rabble-rouser. Pugs are notably calm and well behaved, yet ready to join you in almost any activity. Although Newfoundlands are large and enjoy a good romp (especially if it includes water or kids), they are easygoing and biddable. Some of the other giants, for example, the Saint Bernard, can be surprisingly quiet companions once the sobriety of adulthood sets in. The sight hounds such as the Saluki and Pharaoh Hound have an inborn need to run; if that passion is satisfied, they are contented and mannerly house pets.

Older dogs are not as silly as pups or as filled with the urge to run and jump, punctuating all activities with staccato barks. So if you're sold on having a Vizsla or Welsh Corgi, normally very active dogs, think about finding a retiree (see p. 5).

I'm over seventy and a little slower than I used to be. Can you recommend dogs that would be good for me?

Many people choose a smaller breed to brighten their golden years. A dog lighter than fifteen pounds is easier to carry and empties fewer dog-food bags; cleaning up after her fills up fewer trash bags. Despite these advantages and the obvious asset of your Papillon's fitting so well in your lap, there are disadvantages too. For example, you have to bend or stoop lower to pet her or administer pills. Larger, placid dogs are easier on bad backs, and they are slower on *their* feet too. The care of thick, long coats—or those requiring clipping or "plucking"—must be taken into consideration also, because grooming can be costly or physically taxing.

Dogs that are calm, tractable, easily cared for, and economical are good choices as pets for senior citizens. Adult animals are an option to consider. Dog lovers in their seventies likely have enjoyed—and suffered through—the ups and downs of puppies and don't need or wish to have that experience again. Skipping right over the puddles and chewed slippers to obtain a dog that already knows "Sit" and "Stay" is a bonus. Seniors and retired dogs alike are often grateful for each other's company, giving both new enthusiasm and companionship.

I like the unusual. What would set me off from the rest of the people in the park on Saturday?

Rare breeds are riding a crest of popularity, and those interested in finding the unique have a choice of more than three hundred va-

rieties. Even some AKC breeds are so rare that very few people have heard of them. Among these are the Field Spaniel, Curly-Coated Retriever, Spinone Italiano, and the Chinese Crested, which has only recently joined the Miscellaneous Group.

Other uncommon but obtainable (with some searching) breeds are the Dogue de Bordeaux, Petit Basset Griffon Vendeen, Boykin Spaniel, Coton de Tulear, Polski Owczarek Nizinny, and Peruvian Inca Orchid.

If you want to own the pièce de résistance, you can hire a dog broker to find you a South Russian Owtcharka, Danish Hertha Pointer, Dutch Kooikerhondje, Volpino Italiano, or one of dozens that are entirely unknown in the Western Hemisphere. If you decide to buy one of these rarities, you must be prepared to pay a handsome sum and to undergo a difficult adoption procedure.

Are imports better?

Not necessarily. Some people like to say they have a dog from Germany or Japan or anyplace far away, which may sound impressive to others. In some cases the country of origin has the best quality, but in other instances, the breed was perfected in another country and actually has better stock in its adopted home. One of the greatest disadvantages of importing a dog is that you often have to depend on someone else to make the choice for you.

Professional breeders sometimes import dogs when a small localized gene pool needs new blood or when fitness experts want to restore lost abilities by introducing working stock.

Like wines, dogs include great imports and great domestics—as well as vinegars in both. It's the knowledgeable selection that's important, not the dog's country of origin.

Which kind of dog is the easiest to care for?

Stuffed.

I like Collies, but I don't have time to groom their long hair. Any suggestions?

Smooth Collies are identical to the more familiar Lassie-type Rough variety, except for the coat, which is short and close. Other breeds offer a choice too, such as the Smooth or Wire Fox Terrier; the Longhaired and Smooth Chihuahua; the Smooth, Wire, or Longhaired Dachshund;

and the four varieties of Belgian shepherds: Belgian Sheepdog, Belgian Tervuren, Belgian Malinois, and Belgian Laekenois.

Consider having your dog groomed professionally or clipping the coat shorter. The latter defeats the purpose, though, if the reason you chose the breed was its appearance.

When I was a kid, everybody had a Boston Terrier, but now you hardly see them. What are the most popular breeds?

The top breeds vary with fads, fashion, and finances, from the large, protective breeds to the economical purse size. At one moment, native breeds are the rage, and the next, imports are in mode. Although some buyers want the dog-of-the-hour, dedicated breeders stick by their chosen breeds, staying with them for better or worse.

The media, politics, and world relations have an effect on a breed's popularity, as evidenced by the boom in German Shepherds during the Strongheart and Rin Tin Tin movie era and, conversely, the breed's fall during World War I. Lassie convinced everyone Collies were the best, Benji made hairy dogs appealing, and Disney's Shaggy Dog turned the public on to Old English Sheepdogs. President Franklin Roosevelt's Fala boosted the Scottie's numbers.

Although these statistics change nearly as often as the current hot song, Cockers, Poodles, Labrador and Golden Retrievers, German Shepherds, Chow Chows, Beagles, Miniature Schnauzers, Dachshunds, and Shelties had the most registrations according to the American Kennel Club records of the mid-1980s. For many years the three varieties of Poodles led the pack. Doberman Pinschers and Yorkies are often in the top ten of the hit parade.

My grandfather had a Spitz. Are those still around?

Some of the dogs that were called Spitz were actually specimens of other similar Nordic breeds. The true Spitz, however, is alive, well, and living in various countries around the world, under names such as American Eskimo or Laika. Spitz types are natives of the United States, Japan, Finland, Norway, Sweden, Holland, Germany, and the USSR and are available in sizes extra large to petite. For a time, they had a period of some popularity in the States and then seemed to disappear.

They are now enjoying a resurgence with breeders who delight in their white fluffiness and lively personalities.

I consider myself all-American. What breeds were "Made in the USA"?

More than you think! Coonhound breeds win the race, numbering eight American varieties: Plott Hound, American Blue Gascon Hound, Majestic Tree Hound, American Black and Tan, Bluetick, English, Redbone, and Treeing Walker Coonhounds. American dog lovers also can boast twenty-eight others: Alaskan Malamute, American Bulldog, American Cocker Spaniel, American Eskimo (in three sizes), American Foxhound, American Hairless Terrier, American Pit Bull Terrier, American Staffordshire Terrier, American Water Spaniel, Australian and English Shepherds (despite their names), Black Mouth Cur, Blue Lacy, Boston Terrier, Boykin Spaniel, Carolina Dog (a native pariah), Catahoula Leopard Dog, Chesapeake Bay Retriever, Chinook, Hawaiian Poi Dog (now extinct), Kyi Leo, Leopard Cur, Mountain Cur, Rat Terrier, Siberian Husky, Stephen's Stock, Toy Fox Terrier, and Treeing Tennessee Brindle—all born under the Stars and Stripes.

I'm allergic to dog hair. What breeds don't shed?

Contrary to belief, it is not the hair that causes the allergic reaction, but the dander on the dog's skin. Allergy sufferers should keep the dog as clean as possible. Vacuum both the dog and the house frequently. Do not allow the dog into your bedroom and ask someone else to bathe and brush your pet. If your allergy is severe, it may be necessary to keep him outside.

If it's not an allergy but a distaste for clumps of doggy fuzz wafting about the house, you may want to consider several breeds that have minimal to no shedding. The only breeds that don't shed are the hairless breeds: American Hairless Terrier, Chinese Crested, Peruvian Inca Orchid, Inca Hairless Dog, Xoloitzcuintli, and Mexican Hairless.

Some breeds, however, shed less than others because the hair texture causes the lost hair to stay within the coat. These dogs must be brushed and groomed frequently to avoid tangles and to remove the dead hair. Some of these are the Schnauzer, Poodle, Bichon Frise,

Kerry Blue and Bedlington Terriers, Irish Water Spaniel, Portuguese Water Dog, Soft-Coated Wheaten Terrier, and Bearded Collie. Long-haired dogs don't shed more than smooth-coated breeds—the hair's just longer!

I admire the Greyhound but want something smaller. Are the Whippet and the Italian Greyhound similar to their larger prototype?

The Italian Greyhound is a true Toy, weighing only about eight pounds, and is more fragile than its larger look-alikes. All three are well-behaved dogs reasonably sedate with sufficient exercise, aloof to strangers, and affectionate with their families. In appearance, they are all lean and sleek, with an arched back and folded-back ears. Their speed is legendary, with Greyhounds retaining the title as the swiftest canine, clocked at 45.45 miles per hour!

What is a good apartment dog?

Some apartments or condos stipulate that a dog must be under a certain size. If your landlord is more lenient, large dogs can thrive in close quarters as long as they receive sufficient space to take the kinks out of their legs. A walk down the streets of New York City will prove this when you see Airedale, Boxer, Shepherd, and even Irish Wolfhound owners as well as those walking Maltese, Silkies, and Miniature Dachsies. It has been stated that owners who live in big cities love dogs the most. They must, to wait for the elevator four times (or more) a day, to train their dogs to hold their natural urges until they reach a more

suitable curb, to walk the streets in all kinds of weather looking for the right spot, and to use cleanup equipment and plastic bags.

Certain breeds, such as the Sporting dogs and sight hounds, demand a great deal of exercise, and owners must be prepared to satisfy that need to keep their dogs and themselves content. A Scottish Deerhound that is only taken for a stroll around the block will soon allay his frustrations by clawing through your apartment door or by turning the new coffee table into pick-up sticks.

Most long-term apartment dwellers prefer smaller dogs for convenience and economy of space. Some of these owners paper-train their dogs on tiny porches or balconies, and a few Toy breeds can even be trained to a litter box.

Are Shelties the apartment-size Collie?

Shetland Sheepdogs, or "Shelties," are often advertised in this manner. For Collie lovers who would prefer a dog that is economical to feed and fits easily into a Volkswagen Beetle, the Sheltie is an option. Both breeds are easygoing, affectionate, handsome, and good workers. They differ mainly in color selection, coat (Collies may have smooth coats), and other fine show points, as well as size.

The Sheltie, however, is not simply a "bred-down" version of its larger cousin. Although similar ancestry is certain, other breeds had a part in creating the dog of the Shetland Islands. These small islands produced miniature versions of ponies and sheep, as well as dogs.

We live on a farm. Which breeds are good farm dogs?

Dogs that recognize boundaries! By their nature, Hounds and the Sporting breeds usually run into the next county after a rabbit or bird. All the Herding breeds, many of the Working dogs, and Terriers are excellent farmhands. Pulik, Kelpies, Shelties, Collies, German Shepherds, all varieties of the Belgian shepherds, Welsh Corgis, Bearded Collies, Australian Cattle Dogs, and Australian and English Shepherds all make superb stock-working dogs. The Pyrenees, Komondor, Kuvasz, and other rarer flock-guarding breeds aid in predator control. Terriers, such as the Schnauzer, Rat Terrier, Lakeland Terrier, and others, help keep the farm free of varmints and assist with other chores. In addition, all are good alarm dogs.

What breeds come in varying sizes?

The well-known Poodle is found in Toy, Miniature, and Standard sizes, and Schnauzers offer Miniature, Standard, and Giant choices. Dachshunds have miniatures in all three coat varieties. Bull Terriers have a Toy version and, as mentioned previously, the Spitz is found in various sizes. Others, notably the Beagle, have small variations of an inch or two.

Several dogs have smaller look-alikes in different breeds: Samoyed and Spitz; Doberman Pinscher and Miniature Pinscher; Old English Sheepdog, Bearded Collie, and Nizinny; Greyhound, Whippet, and Italian Greyhound.

How did each breed become distinct?

All dogs were developed to help their owners with various duties: guarding, hauling, herding, hunting, entertainment, pest elimination, and, of course, the most important—companionship. Temperatures of the frozen tundras in the north or the torrid desert regions favored the breeds with longer or shorter coats. Other factors influenced erect or drop ears; rough or waterproof jackets; high, low-set, short, long, or no tails. Through proximity, design, and preference, traits were selected and types were inbred to "fix" breeds.

I'm sure our dogs had a common ancestor, as we do. Did canines descend from wolves?

About the same time that your too-many-to-count-great-grand-fathers were clad in animal skins and hunting the mastodon, dogs

evolved from wolves. Gramps and *Lupus* found that working together
produced full bellies and livened the after-dinner conversation ("Ugh,
Ugh." "Woof!"). As Granny served Masto Hash for the 257th day in
a row, Gramps and his companion could commiserate with each other
and chaw on a shinbone.

What is the newest breed of dog in the United States?

It seems as if there is a new breed introduced every month. By the
time this book is published, three or four others will have appeared.
Nevertheless, some of the most recent immigrants are the Dutch Shepherd, Karst Shepherd, Tosa Inu, Lundehund, and Karelian Bear Dog.

I'd like to show my dog. Which breeds are the easiest to show and which are the most difficult?

It depends on what you consider difficult: complicated grooming,
athletic ability and stamina, handling a dog that's stronger than you
are, or competing against large numbers. Dog show exhibitors must
learn to take their losses. No breeds are easy to finish to a Championship.

If you can learn to take your lumps with the rest of us, the most
numerous breeds—Afghans, Doberman Pinschers, German Shepherds, Golden Retrievers, Siberian Huskies, and Irish Setters—have
stiff competition. These same breeds require a handler who has good
lungs and leg power. Showing the less common breeds, such as Harriers,
Sussex or Field Spaniels, American Water Spaniels, or Curly-Coated
Retrievers, can also be difficult because competition is difficult to find.
Soft-Coated Wheaten Terriers, Poodles, and Scotties are among those
that need knowledgeable grooming. Of course, novices can and do win
even with these "toughies."

For the newcomer, a middle-of-the-road breed may be a good
choice. Some good examples are German Shorthaired Pointers, Nor-
wegian Elkhounds, Schipperkes, Vizslas, and Bullmastiffs. Many others
would suit a beginner. Attend several dog shows, observe the variety,
find some breeds you like, and follow up with questions to the exhibitors.
It is not a good idea to choose a dog on the basis of showing statistics
alone.

If you're a poor sport at losing, this is the wrong game for you.
Better stick to solitaire; then you have only yourself to blame.

What colors do dogs come in?

Dogs offer a better color selection than Gloria Vanderbilt: black, white, gray, blue, red, orange, yellow, or brown. All of these are available in various shades and markings—stripes, solids, tweeds, spots, and mixtures.

Buyers should remember, though, color is one of the least important qualities when choosing a dog. If your pet bites your kids or is sickly, it doesn't make any difference whether he matches your designer living room. Nevertheless, if you have two pups to choose from that perfectly fit your requirements, color may be a final consideration.

3

Paper Chase

What can I name my dog?

AKC allows the use of any acceptable name or combination of names that is twenty-five letters or fewer. No numbers, obscenities, or disparaging names will be approved. In addition, the choice may not include common "doggy" lingo such as *dog*, *bitch*, *dam*, or *runt*; terms such as *Champion* or *Winner*; all or portions of breed names (Polly Pug or Billy Beagle); or the name of a famous living (or recently deceased) person. The registration application blank specifies that the name should be unusual (to avoid duplications) and gives you space for a second choice, should your first selection be turned down. Rejection of the dog's proposed name can happen if you choose an unacceptable one or a kennel name that has been registered with the club for exclusive use.

CKC has the same restrictions, with the additional exclusion of the royal family names, that is, no Princess Di or Jolly Prince Cholly. They allow thirty spaces.

UKC stipulates similar restrictions: no awards or titles, no lewd or offensive names, no abbreviations. Their registration process differs in that a name must have two parts and must not have more than twenty-two letters and spaces. For instance, if an application made out for Buck arrives, the registry will give the dog your last name, that is, Miller's Buck. No two dogs may be registered with the same name, so if you wish to name your pup after its sire or dam, you must give it a Roman numeral, that is, Smith's Rowdy II. Another acceptable choice would be a combination of their names: Smith's Rowdy Dinah. When a breeder fills out a litter registration application for UKC, she includes the name, sex, color, date of birth, and sire/dam with their registration numbers. She is then sent puppy registration certificates, green forms that have a bill of sale on the back for transfer to the buyer.

A good suggestion is to use your last name or to make up a "kennel" name in conjunction with your other choice. For instance, if you've decided to call your Irish Terrier Kelly, you may want to select an Irish-sounding name with it, such as O'Keefe. You can also choose Eringobragh's Kelly or an appropriate regional description, that is, Kelly O'Greenlane. Or you may decide to combine your children's names— Kimjac's Kelly—or go for something really unique: Leapin' Leprechaun's Kelly.

Must I use the seller's choice?

If the breeder has already printed a name on the blue application, the buyer may legally change it, as the owner has the privilege of naming the dog. It is considered poor etiquette by most breeders, however, and may jeopardize your relationship with the seller. Changing the pup's name without the breeder's knowledge and approval may confuse his records and may even nullify your contract. Any disagreement should be discussed at the time of purchase.

Breeders who wish others to know they bred the dog usually put their kennel and a call name on the registration application that accompanies a pup. In fact, prenamed pups are a good indication of "pride in product." Often breeders use an alphabetical or categorical system in naming their pups: The first litter may be called Ammo, Alleluia, Amazing, and so on, with Beautiful Dreamer, Breezy, and Bliss in the second litter. Or, as an alternative, Bentley, Jaguar, Peugeot, Ferrari; or Harvard, Dartmouth, Rutgers, Bryn Mawr, and Sarah Lawrence.

If you have a strong desire for a different name, talk it over with the breeder. He may decide to let you choose the name or to make a compromise, such as keeping his kennel name and beginning with a certain letter, that is, Bigshot's N—. If you are adamant about naming the pup yourself and the breeder equally determined, you may find yourself at a stalemate. You may then find it advantageous to make your purchase elsewhere. It just depends on what's more important to you—the registered name or this particular pup.

I don't like the name the breeder gave her; can I change it?

Once the application has been approved and AKC has issued a registration certificate for an individual dog, the name is irrevocable. For a price and a court appearance, you can change *your* name, but not your dog's. You may call her whatever you want as a nickname; however, you must use her complete registered name whenever you participate in any activities that are under the jurisdiction of the kennel club, such as breeding, showing, or selling her.

UKC does allow the new owner to change the name when ownership is transferred, until the dog has attained a title. The breeder may also cross out that option on the certificate if he has a signed bill of sale that states no name change will be allowed.

Why is my Bouvier named Duchess XXIII?

This simply means there are twenty-two other AKC-registered Bouviers named Duchess. Only thirty-seven dogs of each breed may receive the same name, and AKC attaches the Roman numeral suffix.

Can I give my new pup the same name as my old Affenpinscher, who died recently?

To enable you to reuse a name and to assist the registry body in maintaining records to date, notify the kennel club when a dog dies. Mark the registration paper "deceased" across the front and send it to the kennel club. It may be possible for you to honor your old dog's memory if the maximum number has not been reached, as discussed previously.

Why should I register Inky, and where can I do this?

Registered dogs may be shown in conformation, obedience, field events, or tracking trials and may compete for titles. Pups of registered animals are also eligible for registration, making Inky and his progeny more valuable financially. If you believe you will ever show, breed, or sell your pet, you should register him. In addition, a registration certificate made out in your name establishes proof of ownership. The American Kennel Club and Canadian Kennel Club register litters out of registered dogs and individual pups from these litters. Information and forms may be obtained from AKC.

United Kennel Club also registers eligible litters and the individual pups. If the dog is purebred, meets the requirements, and the sire and/or dam is not registered, owners may request a Single Dog Registration (see p. 37). Kennel clubs are listed in Helpful Addresses, page 187.

What are "papers"? Which should I expect to receive with my purchase?

The term *papers* often is believed to show that the dog is registered, although, in reality, it may refer to any papers given with the pup— from the pedigree to the receipt, or the newspapers spread on the floor for housebreaking.

If you have bought a registered pup, the least you should receive are medical records, the registration application or certificate, and a bill of sale or contract. A pedigree is often included, and it is wise to ask whether there is any guarantee relating to health and/or show faults as well. If your pup is a mixed breed or is from unregistered stock, it is unlikely that the breeder will offer any of these bonuses. Do ask, however, for a receipt and a record of shots, worming, and physical examination.

What is the difference between a blue slip and a white slip? AKC wrote to me saying that I need a transfer form. What is that?

The blue paper is the registration application, on which you apply for your dog's name and for ownership. It also records your dog's sex, color and markings, sire, dam, litter number, and date of birth. Once you have sent in the form (blue) with the appropriate fee and it is accepted, you will receive your dog's permanent registration certificate (white). This white paper shows ownership and gives the individual registration number and the dog's description. This accompanies the dog if it is resold.

A transfer slip must be attached to the certificate if the dog has changed hands more than once between registrations of ownership. This can occur in a pet shop purchase, or when a pup is sold to a buyer who is suddenly unable to keep the dog and returns it to the seller, who then sells the dog to you.

UKC's puppy registration certificates are green and have to be sent in only upon change of ownership.

I found a puppy that I like, but the breeder wants to "withhold" the papers. Is that OK?

If your primary interest is to obtain a companion and you do not plan to show your dog or to breed it, a mutual agreement between the buyer and the seller can stipulate this fact. As long as you both agree in writing, you can still have the puppy that you want. Conscientious breeders may want to save both you and themselves embarrassment if the dog would be disqualified in the show ring. Examples could be a white Shepherd, a "fluffy" Welsh Pembroke Corgi, or a bobtailed Australian Cattle Dog, none of which meets Standard requirements. Not all owners are interested in showing or breeding, and these dogs can still give and receive love and friendship.

Armstrong is purebred but doesn't have papers. Can I still register him?

You have two options. If the sire and dam were listed and you are able to obtain the complete name and numbers of both, you can apply to the proper registration authority. The kennel club will inform you as to the process necessary to obtain registration. Or you can apply for an Individual Listing Privilege (ILP) with AKC. The UKC has a similar provision, the Single Dog Registration.

How do I obtain an ILP on my dog?

Write to the proper officials and ask for the appropriate form. Complete the blank and return it with the fee. If the application is rejected, the fee will be returned. The ILP blank asks for information about the appearance of the dog, the breeding (if known), the basis on which the owner believes it to be purebred, and the reason it is not registerable. This may cover dogs that are found or obtained from an animal shelter. It is helpful to have experts in the breed (exhibitors, handlers, veterinarians, or members of kennel clubs) write a note stating their opinion about the purity of the dog.

Two recent color photographs of your dog must accompany the application. One must be from the front and the other a profile, both full views of the dog in a standing position.

The dog must be more than six months of age at the time of application. (UKC's Single Dog Registration requires that dogs be one year or more.) If your dog is granted an ILP, you may show him at AKC obedience trials and earn titles. It does not, however, permit your dog to be shown in conformation or to breed a registered litter. All progeny of an ILP parent must go through the same process.

I still haven't received the registration papers on my pup, and it's been over a month. What can I do?

If a dog is advertised as registered, *do not* buy him without receiving either the registration application, registration certificate, or (if the papers are still in transit) a contract giving complete information needed to obtain the papers. A breeder of AKC dogs is required to keep records and furnish the required data. Your bill of sale should include the following:

> Breed, sex, and color of dog
> Date of birth
> Registered names and numbers of sire and dam
> Name of breeder

Processing takes about three weeks, so wait about a month, then call the seller to see whether she has received notification. If she is a reliable breeder, she is probably concerned herself and can phone the registration department at AKC. If you feel she is misleading you, contact AKC and send them photocopies of your check and the bill of sale, and the authorities will take appropriate steps. Without this information, nothing can be done. This is one of AKC's biggest headaches and, of course, it also is for the buyer who expects to receive registration papers.

Are pedigreed and purebred the same thing?

A *pedigree* is simply a list of ancestors. Naturally, everybody has ancestors, whether or not they're pure Chinese, Australian, Chinese Shar Pei, or Australian Terrier. Even if they're part Aussie and part Shar Pei, they still have parents and grandparents.

Purebred means that the dog is a 100 percent bona fide, gen-u-wine specimen of one breed and one breed only.

Is a pedigree like a family tree? Why should I care whether there is a CH in the pedigree? I don't plan to show.

A pedigree is precisely a family tree, whether it's the sire and dam typed on a piece of paper or a fancy six-generation pedigree on parchment, showing all 126 of your dog's ancestors.

Whether or not they plan to show, buyers want a sturdy, happy representative of the breed, and they want their Scottie to look like a Scottie, not a Cairn or Norwich Terrier. Titles such as Champion, Hunting Retriever Champion, and Utility Dog indicate that the ancestor was a high-quality example of the breed and demonstrated that fact in competition for conformation, obedience, and/or ability awards. These grand-sounding appellations also imply mental and physical soundness of the titled dog, because at least a minimal amount of stability and stamina are required for competition.

All I received was the names of the mother and the father. Can I obtain a more complete pedigree?

If the sire and dam were registered, you can write to the appropriate registry body or an individual pedigree service, giving all pertinent information (names, birthdates, registration numbers if available). The kennel clubs and services can furnish five-, six-, or even seven-generation pedigrees for a nominal fee. UKC provides a complimentary three-generation pedigree with registration certificates.

How do I read a pedigree? What are all these mystic abbreviations: CD, CDX, HIT, ROM?

All the abbreviations stand for titles and awards received from the kennel clubs and the national specialty (parent) clubs. Several are given in the Glossary (pp. 185–86).

Reading a pedigree tells the novice who the ancestors of the dog are. For the discerning, however, it tells much, much more, especially when it is a complete pedigree. Many breeders or services list colors of the ancestors; these give an idea of inheritance and of possible results in future breedings.

Titles show competence in various areas: for example, a great many advanced obedience titles show intelligence in the lines; conformation Championships indicate correct physical attributes. Other titles can show abilities or instincts, many of which are heritable. Duplication of names shows linebreeding or inbreeding.

Someone who is truly knowledgeable of bloodlines can also make an educated guess on a proposed breeding from studying the pedigrees. She may know whether the line is predominant in producing coats that are long or short; wiry, curly, wavy, or straight; tight or plush. The expert can predict which attributes and faults to expect.

The breeder where I bought my pup had me sign an agreement to neuter/spay. Why?

This is a common practice if the breeder feels strongly that the puppy should not be bred. The owner of the litter may sell all pet-quality puppies with that stipulation, trying to do his part in controlling animal overpopulation. It is also possible that the dog has a fault that could be passed to its progeny. Although oversize, missing teeth, or poor markings will not affect your dog as a pet, such a trait means he will not be an asset to a breeding program.

What if I change my mind later and want to breed her?

Written agreements are legal and binding. A court of law could force you to spay her. In one instance, a buyer finished the Championship of a bitch named in a spay agreement. The judge upheld the contract, and the Champion bitch was spayed despite her quality and the considerable funds spent in showing her. If you feel you may change your mind, do not sign such an agreement. Instead look for another dog; then no one feels cheated. Be prepared, however; people usually charge a correspondingly higher price for breeding stock.

What kind of contract should I receive?

All the information given on the registration application should be reiterated on the contract for identification purposes. Most sellers suggest that the buyer have the animal examined by a veterinarian and allow ample time (usually about forty-eight hours) to return the dog during that period. The contract often includes any other guarantees and/or restrictions agreed to by both parties. This should then be dated and signed by both of you. Read the contract thoroughly (including the fine print), and ask questions about any clause you don't understand.

What is a guarantee? What good are health and show guarantees?

No one can guarantee your puppy will be perfect, just as your obstetrician cannot promise you a healthy infant. This is a risk we take in purchases; sometimes unfortunate circumstances occur. The guarantee is only as good as the seller's integrity. This is why finding a breeder with a spotless reputation is important. Reputable breeders who give guarantees often charge more for a dog than those who sell their stock "as is."

Although a guarantee cannot make your puppy's cataract recede or your show prospect's bite perfect, you may be able to receive some compensation for your heartbreak. Health and show guarantees usually cover only serious problems such as crippling defects or faults defined as disqualifying or serious in the breed Standard for a period of time, usually up to one year. The breeder cannot cover minor, though frustrating situations such as chronic ear infections or improper coat texture. Environment, as well as heredity, can affect a dog's growth and development, and unexplained problems can appear. A mistreated or neglected pup will not glow with health or exhibit a sparkling personality.

What is a "replacement"?

Although one dog can never truly replace another that you have loved, replacements are often a breeder's method of trying to compensate you for a loss. Your dog may be replaced with one of equal value if this clause is in your contract.

The breeder wants to sell me a dog with all sorts of strings attached. I'd like to think Champ's mine when I pay for her. What do you think?

Breeders sometimes put stipulations on the sale when they feel the dog is of exceptional quality or they are giving you a lower price than usual. Discuss any contract clauses that you consider unfair or unreasonable. Perhaps you can reach a compromise.

For instance, if the pup you are buying is show quality and the contract requires it to be shown, but you don't wish to show, you may choose another pup from the litter. If the seller is eager to place the pup, she may agree to drop the request or to show the puppy for you.

If you cannot agree, look elsewhere for your Champ. Do not sign anything you don't intend to uphold, as broken agreements cause hard feelings and sometimes lead to lawsuits.

I received a wad of papers with my pup. What do all these things mean?

Experienced breeders save themselves from midnight phone calls by answering questions before they're asked. To do this, they insert printed information into the puppy packet sent home with the buyers. At the very least you should receive a pedigree, a contract or bill of sale, the registration paper, and a medical record of shots and worming, with any other pertinent information such as heartworm preventive. There should be instructions on feeding and essential grooming. You may also find directions on housebreaking and crate training. Extra niceties are a list of suggested books to read, names of local training classes and clubs, data on the national organization, and a copy of the breed Standard. A really efficient seller will include a copy of this book!

4

A Feast Fit for King

Should I feed King dry food or canned? How about table scraps? What about the moist packs and the gravy foods?

Because dogs don't brush after every meal, they need abrasive stimulation to their gums and teeth. Feeding dry food helps keep King's teeth clean, whereas a diet consisting only of meat is bad for him. If you wish to mix in canned meat or a taste of your leftovers, he'll love it. An occasional potato, leftover linguine, or a piece of fried fish can make his dinner a banquet for one night. Just don't go overboard. Too many extras can upset his stomach and digestion.

The moist packs are high in salt and not recommended as a regular diet, particularly for older dogs. Because these packs are convenient, store compactly, and don't spoil, however, they are handy for traveling. Most people love gravy, and so do most dogs. Gravy foods are a treat, as leftovers are, but unnecessary.

When you feed a good-quality dry food with a side bowl of water, you'll be providing King with everything necessary. Dogs' eating preferences aren't like ours; they don't need or even want the variety we crave. Some pets refuse to eat or become picky if you change their food.

I get confused standing at the dog food aisle. There are so many brands and varieties. Which should I choose?

Just be glad your dog doesn't eat cereal! Ask the breeder and your veterinarian for suggestions. Unless you're a pro with knowledge of the varieties, you'd better buy a name brand. If you only buy four-star poultry and prime or Grade A meat for your family, can you do any less for its four-legged member? The major brands of dog food contain all the ingredients a healthy dog needs.

Keep in mind pets don't need fancy packages or the beef-red color or any of the gewgaws given a lot of hoopla by advertisers. The dog isn't attracted by red color; the owner is.

Should I add supplements to the food? Should I add vitamin C to prevent bone disease? I've heard that a tablespoon of apple cider vinegar added to the food keeps away the fleas.

A healthy dog needs no supplements if you are feeding her good-quality food. Some breeders give vitamins to puppies, particularly those of the fast-growing breeds. It is best not to fool around with additives, because the wrong ingredient can upset the correct balance. Too much calcium can cause growth disorders, for instance. Vitamin C has not been medically proved to prevent or cure anything. It also does no harm, so if you wish to attempt to cure your dog's winking her left eye with a dose of vitamin C, go ahead and try. Just don't hold your breath.

Some owners swear by vinegar. A heavy infestation of fleas, however, will suck acid blood as well as sweet. Again, these products in moderation do not harm your dog, and if you wish to try a natural debugger, good luck!

I can hardly stand the smell of some dog foods. Any suggestions?

Some are definite nose-wrinklers, especially the bargain brands of canned meat and meat by-products. Many of the new stews do not have the strong odor. If the smell is really offensive to you, stay with the dry foods; they have little odor and are nutritious. Just remember that what smells awful to you may be Kennel No. 5 to your dog.

What about generic food?

The generic food labels specify that they are not suggested for puppies or for pregnant, active, or ill dogs. Those that are left are the silent minority, silent because they can't complain, not until their bodies do it for them. Don't take chances; stick to reputable quality. Some generic products are fine, but save your money on envelopes or paper towels instead, not something that affects your dog's health.

I don't believe commercial dog food is good enough for my dog. I'd like to feed Rebel a home-cooked, balanced meal. Where can I find proportions and recipes?

Some books on dogs include recipes for your pet, and magazines such as *Dog World, Dog Fancy*, and *Pure-Bred Dogs/American Kennel Gazette* occasionally feature canine home cookin'. You may try writing to the editor of one of these magazines, asking her to publish your request in the letters to the editor. These magazines are available on newsstands and at dog shows. Dog clubs occasionally publish cookbooks that have a section with canine cuisine.

In the meantime, you can jazz up Rebel's life with some cuts from the butcher's. Your dog won't care what it is. Rebel will enjoy liver, chicken, or hamburger as much as steak. In fact, he'd love intestines, lungs, chicken necks (boned), or butcher-saw scraps. Introduce these products slowly, as they may be too rich, causing Rebel to decorate your carpet in appreciation of your efforts.

Princess only likes white meat of chicken, boiled, if you please. When I try feeding her anything else, she won't eat. I'm afraid she'll starve.

It's if *you* please, and fussing pleases her. Dogs will take anything they can sweet talk you into. Would you allow a child to eat only coq au vin? Of course not! Most people do not have time to cater to demands for fancy cooking. You'd tell your son to eat his pancakes and stop whining!

Talk to a veterinarian about this problem and ask how long Princess can keep her nose in the air and her jaws clenched tightly. Then harden your heart and stick to the vet's recommendation. Put down her bowl of dry food, perhaps with a bit of meat. In fifteen minutes, pick it up and continue with your daily routine. Do that daily—no cheating! Princess won't starve. It may take a few days, but soon she'll climb off her throne and join the rest of the common folk.

When I brought my puppy home, the breeder said she was feeding him Brand X puppy food. My other dog eats Brand Y. Do I have to buy two kinds, or can I switch one of them?

It's best to keep a young dog on puppy food for most of the first year. After that period, you can change one or the other or both of your dogs to the same product. But you can change your new dog to the puppy food made by Brand Y. Make any changes slowly so that you do not upset digestion or taste preferences. Start by mixing a small bit of the new brand with the old into his dish and increasing the proportion daily.

When should I feed? Does it hurt Gus if I'm a little late or early feeding him? How about free choice versus regular meals?

Once Gus is an adult, you may choose to feed him in the morning or evening. It's best to have a routine: when you have your own dinner, for instance. It won't be harmful if the schedule varies a few hours once in a while, when you will not be at home during his regular time.

Free-choice meals equal free-choice stools and make a dog hard to housebreak. The only advantage of free choice is for the owner, because this method allows you to fill the bowl every day (or two or three), depending on how much Gus eats. Of course, free choice must be dry meal, with no meat or water added because the food could spoil over a period of time.

Schatzie picks at his food all day. It drives me nuts! At 2:00 A.M., I still hear crunching.

You've established a bad habit. Skip a meal, so Schatzie will be feeling the pangs of hunger when you feed him. If Schatzie hasn't finished in fifteen minutes, pick up the bowl, and don't give him any more until the following day. He'll soon learn to lick the bowl clean, right down to the picture of Jack Sprat on the bottom.

How often do I feed? When should I cut my puppy back from four meals a day to three, and three to two? Should I feed one or two meals to an adult?

When puppies are first weaned from their mother, they are fed four small meals a day. As they are able to consume more at one sitting, the total food is increased and divided into three meals by the time the puppy goes to her new home. When you are feeding a litter of ten Great Danes, the amount in the community pan is staggering!

The food consumption escalates quickly, and, by about six months of age, the puppy is eating seemingly enormous dinners and can flourish on two meals per day. Often dogs start ignoring or nibbling at one meal, allowing you to eliminate that feeding. Some time around puberty (seven to eight months for Toy breeds, twelve to fourteen for giants, and ten to twelve months for others), the appetite begins to decrease a bit, and an owner can make a choice of giving one large meal or dividing the day's requirement into two feedings. A hint: dogs seem to gain more on two meals a day, so this is a good choice if your young adult could stand a few pounds. If she's already a "chubbette," once a day may be preferable.

My Poodle, Buckley, doesn't eat as much as the directions on the dog food bags suggest. How do I know how much to feed him?

Ask the breeder of your Poodle how much her adults eat. Perhaps Buckley's relatives are "easy keepers" (dogs who thrive on less food than the average). Check your dog's appearance, both by looks and by feel.

Buckley should be sturdy to the touch with a slight padding over the ribs, not feather-pillow plump or skeleton thin. Watch him to see whether he is lively, ready to play and take walks. You may want to check with your veterinarian to make sure nothing is wrong, particularly if your pet appears listless or extremely thin or has a dull coat or eyes.

The amounts listed on the dog food bags are only averages, and we all know dogs are no more average than their owners!

What is the perfect weight? How can I tell whether my dog is too fat?

Certainly, what looks good on a Chihuahua would make a Bulldog look anorexic. Like the human's "spare tire," a dimple and roll just in front of the tail tell us when a dog's becoming more than pleasantly plump. If you can you pinch an inch, he's too fat! Ask your vet or breeder if you're unsure.

How can Sweets be too fat? She only eats a half can of food a day.

This is rather like an old joke: Husband says, "How can I be fat? I only eat one meal a day." Wife answers, "Yes, you start at 7:00 A.M. and finish at 10:00 P.M."

A half can may be too much if it's king-size and your dog is tiny or one whose daily activity consists of walking to the food bowl. Keep track of a typical day. Do you let Sweets finish your milk and cereal after breakfast? Does she share the cat's meal? How many times does she bark at the cookie jar and you give her a treat without even knowing it?

Should I feed Tiffany when she begs? What kind of treats can I give her? I've heard sugar will give her worms.

Giving in to those soulful looks can shorten Tiffany's life as well as encourage a bad habit. One or two dog treats before bed or when you're having a snack is OK. A couple of pieces of popcorn tossed into the air for her to catch and crunch won't hurt her. Go ahead and give Tiffany a bit of cheese or half a slice of leftover bacon as a treat after breakfast now and then. Keep an eye on her waist and use common sense about how much and how often.

Sugar will not produce worms, but it adds no quality to her diet. One piece of cake on her tenth birthday (if she's healthy, of course) won't cost her an eleventh birthday, but indulgence shouldn't be a regular habit.

Dogs don't know what they're missing. They don't start salivating at a picture of a hot fudge sundae. They only want to eat because you are eating.

You can try feeding your pet at the same time as you eat and be firm about allowing no begging. After all, you don't beg for his food; why should he be allowed to ask for yours?

When I was a kid, Rover always had a bone to gnaw. Now I hear they're not good for dogs, so I haven't given Rover-ette any. She has a terrific nose for them in the trash, though. What if she accidentally swallows one?

Cooked bones should never be given; small chop or poultry bones can splinter. Those from round steaks have been caught around a dog's jaw or stuck in the throat, so care must be taken with the round bones. Large uncooked bones, such as a beef knuckle, can be enjoyed by Roverette and have the bonus effect of cleaning her teeth.

Dogs can sniff out a leftover pork chop or half-eaten drumstick for a mile, it seems, and sometimes persistence pays off for them. If you find Roverette guiltily munching the remains of a carcass, feed her some bread. This protects the stomach as the shards pass through. The main dangers are intestinal impaction and sharp edges tearing tender linings. Of course, bread is not even in the same ballpark as bones for taste, so spread it with something appealing such as liver sausage. Peanut butter works great: even if she won't eat it immediately, it'll stick to the roof of her mouth until she gives in and swallows!

Will garlic kill worms?

No, it only wards off vampires.

Garlic has no therapeutic effect, although dogs adore the taste of it. Adding a bit of garlic powder to cooked liver or to homemade treats spices up your dog's life.

How much water does Jiffy need?

Jiffy should have access to fresh, cold water at all times. This is especially important during hot weather to prevent dehydration. Limiting water can have disastrous effects, particularly for dogs with kidney problems.

Does a neutered dog become fat?

The only effect neutering has is eliminating the possibility of reproduction. The excess calories that were used during matings, pregnancies, whelpings, and nursing are no longer needed. Because most dogs are neutered at maturity, the surgery often coincides with completion of growth and a decrease in activity, all of which requires less food. Some owners fail to take all this into consideration and continue to feed the same meals they fed their active pup. Before you know it, the dog has to start aerobics or sign up at the local diet club.

Does an older dog need less or different food?

Senior dogs are often less active and require smaller meals with less protein. Sometimes they prefer having their portions divided into two or three snacks, rather than the full banquets they enjoyed as youngsters. Health changes such as heart disease or kidney problems must be considered. Softened food may be needed for a dog who has lost teeth.

If your "golden oldie" has lost her appetite, you may try to spark it up a bit by heating her meal or adding a sprinkle of garlic powder or some other goody she adores. Watch her figure and consult your vet if you notice a severe weight loss or too many extra pounds.

Do you feed an outdoor dog more than one who lives indoors?

If your pet is extremely active outdoors, you may find it necessary to increase his food. Professional breeders often augment meals for kennel residents during cold weather, because dogs burn extra calories in freezing temperatures.

My vet suggested putting Hans on "K/D" or kidney-diet food. It's awfully expensive! Is this really necessary?

People whose doctors recommend special diets can shop and cook carefully. But dog foods are sold already "cooked and mixed," with most store brands being basically the same.

When a medical condition requires specific dietary changes for Hans, the choices are cooking up the menu yourself or buying one of these specialized foods. These prescription brands may be a bit more expensive than regular dog food, but they can help save on medical bills while allowing Hans a longer and more trouble-free life.

Diets are available that are low in protein for dogs with kidney insufficiency, low in salt for heart patients, and high in bland digestibility for stomach and intestinal problems. Specific foods can dissolve bladder stones, help dogs with food allergies, or aid overweight dogs to diet. Others are especially formulated for dogs experiencing the stress of pregnancy and lactation or running long hours in field trials or sled races.

5

How to Build a Better Doghouse

What kind of doghouse should my new puppy have, and where should I put it?

Not in the "back forty," please! Put his home close enough to yours so that you can see him and he can participate in family activities. As you go out the back door toward the garage for work, call "Hi, Scratch!" and give him a pat on the head. After school, the kids can play a game and Scratch can join in the fun. Come Saturday, you and Scratch can keep up a running conversation as you pull the weeds from the garden. The closer a dog is to you geographically, the closer he will be emotionally.

Your dog's home can be fancy or plain. Simple plywood will do, although you can insulate it or customize by adding air-conditioning or solar heat, if you wish. The floor should be raised off the ground for protection from the cold and damp. Face the house or kennel toward the south if possible to ward off cold wintry gusts. A house with a partition, similar to the one in the drawing (p. 54), will protect the dog from the elements. When planning, don't make the "bedroom" too large; body heat is conserved in cozy quarters when the dog curls up, creating his own insulation. Top it off with a hinged or removable roof that can be lifted for easier cleaning.

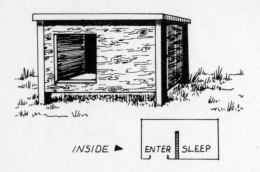

INSIDE ▶   ENTER ┃ SLEEP

What is the best bedding for an outside dog?

Wood shavings are great, particularly cedar chips if you can find them. They stay dry and help eliminate doggy odor. Indoor/outdoor carpeting, which allows you to slip in a new piece when shampooing the other, is a good choice also. Blankets are acceptable, but they become soiled easily and must be changed regularly. Conversely, newspaper and straw are poor choices (wet straw stinks!) and only better than no bedding at all. They become wet and dirty quickly and should be changed at least once a day. No floor covering is necessary in hot weather, although wood shavings aid in cleanliness.

I'd like to leave Heidi outside while I'm at work, bringing her inside at night and when it's cold. Will that be harmful?

Many families prefer to keep the family pet outdoors in the daytime to protect their homes and to provide their dog an opportunity for outdoor exercise. Changing from air-conditioning to torrid temperatures or from a heated home to polar days, however, can be a trial for a pet. Nevertheless, if the temperature change is not too extreme, Heidi will enjoy your company indoors in the evening.

What kind of confinement should I use in the house? I think crates are cruel!

Even though some people think of crates as a punishment, most pets find security and peace in them. Canines are den creatures. Believe it or not, they look upon their crates as their "rooms," entering them willingly. Some pets open the door, go inside, and close the door after themselves!

Crates are the safest, surest confinement, ensuring that neither the dog nor the house will meet disaster in your absence. If you prefer, however, you can erect a pen in your basement or garage for times when you are gone, or an unfinished room can serve as your dog's own place.

Crates are not cruel. Coming home to a torn drape, puddles on the rugs, or a chewed table leg, all of which may be followed by yelling at and beating your dog—*that* is cruel.

What choices do I have for confining Maggie when she's outside?

Erecting a kennel run or fencing your yard (or a portion of it) is the best protective measure for Maggie. They help eliminate the problems associated with dogs' roaming loose. Fences should be tall enough so that your dog won't be able to jump or scramble over them. Some owners take advantage of a garage wall for one side of the pen. If Maggie is a climber, put a top on the kennel or line the fence with thick bushes. Chain-link is the "coop de grace" of the fence world; it's the sturdiest and most weather-resistant.

Tying or chaining a dog is not recommended by experts, although it is a better alternative than allowing her to run at large. A dog that is tied has limited protection from tormentors or severe weather. Tied dogs tend to become aggressive if teased. Make sure Maggie has a safe house or hideaway for protection.

Is it better to keep Sheba inside or outside?

In this case, absence does not make the heart grow fonder. Research shows dogs that live inside homes become the best friends and protectors of their family and its property. Indoor pets develop more personality and intelligence through the social contact. You will miss sharing 90 percent of your dog's life if she lives outdoors.

Yet it's the quality of the time you spend with her, not the quantity, that matters most. If you're gone all day, scheduling regular periods for you and Sheba to enjoy each other's company will strengthen your relationship. Don't let your only time together be feeding, cleaning up, and performing other chores. Train Sheba, take her for a walk or car ride, play ball, or take her hunting.

Shouldn't my dog have the freedom to roam?

When it comes to animals, freedom is not all it's cracked up to be. Loose dogs become delinquent dogs. Strays rummage through the neighbors' garbage, defecate in annoying places, come home pregnant, run away, chase farm animals, transmit disease, kill cats, bite kids, and starve. These are the dogs that are poisoned, exposed to bad weather, hit by cars, and picked up by animal control officers to be euthanized. They are the dogs that help make up the tragic statistics. National statistics show that 15 million dogs are brought to shelters each year, out of which about 11 million are humanely destroyed; an additional 7 million meet their end while experiencing "freedom."

I've been advised to buy crates. I like to let Muggs and Jethro ride loose. Give me one reason why I should cage them. What other uses do crates have?

One reason? Safety—yours and theirs. Dogs riding loose have caused accidents by climbing all over their owners at inopportune times. When they are confined in crates, pets are unable to jump out of moving vehicles or to stick their heads out of windows, as they *love* to do. This bad habit can cause severe eye injuries.

There are more advantages. If you leave the car, you can roll down your windows with no danger of a runaway. Crated dogs can be removed

from a stuffy vehicle and placed under a nearby shady tree while you picnic. Most important, on the road, crates protect your canine friends in case of an accident.

In addition to safety, crates are great for use as a drying room after baths or a run through mud puddles. They're indispensable house-breaking aids (see p. 66) and work well as grooming tables. You can separate your dogs during meals, so Jethro doesn't eat Muggs's pill and so that greedy Muggs doesn't gobble all of Jethro's food.

Furthermore, crates prevent your dogs from doing damage to your home while you're away. Airlines require them for shipping pets. They serve as enforced separation during heat cycles. And that's not all: they make roomy end tables!

What can I use to protect Blitz's outdoor pen from the sun and to keep snow out?

Many kennel owners use corrugated fiberglass roofing. It is inexpensive and may be bought in green, which helps reflect the sun's rays. In addition, you can plant bushes near Blitz's kennel run or erect a privacy fence blocking sun and snow. Hang tarps and lower them during heavy winds and blowing snow. If you live in an area that receives a great deal of snow, it's a good idea to use a kennel door with a snow panel, which allows you to open the door above the drifts (and, as a bonus, helps keep puppies inside).

I'd like to build a really nice kennel building. Where do I start? What is the best footing?

Begin by selecting an area convenient for you, but away from neighbors. Then check your zoning laws.

Cement, patio blocks, sand, and pea gravel work as well as flooring. Most people who have more than one dog choose cement because it is the easiest to clean and disinfect. It needs a rough surface, however, to eliminate slippery-when-wet situations. Patio blocks—much cheaper than poured cement—follow close behind for easy care. If closely butted together and cemented, they can be a good choice. Both cement and blocks have the disadvantage of sometimes creating bone problems such as weak pasterns or splayed feet.

Sand and pea gravel help produce nice, tight feet and strong pasterns. Either footing is inexpensive but must be replaced regularly. With these surfaces, it is more difficult to eradicate odors completely or to sterilize against parasites, viruses, and bacteria.

Decide what kind of a building you'd like; then determine what's affordable. Kennels can be as expensive as second homes or may be constructed by the owner, a bit at a time. Chain-link fencing is a must, with indoor/outdoor runs large enough to allow for ample exercise. You will need to choose roofing, door styles, beds or platforms, width and length of pens, feeding and watering stations. Decisions must be made about heat, plumbing, air-conditioning, septic disposal, grooming facilities, whelping room, and privacy panels between runs. Check with the Board of Health for the proper setup regarding waste disposal. Consult books and magazine features for additional options and ideas.

My dog sleeps inside, so I don't have to worry about outdoor buildings, but should she have her own place?

She should be trained to sleep wherever *you* want her to—in a crate, in a doggy basket, on a blanket beside your bed, or at your son's feet.

What gear do I have to have as soon as I bring my dog home?

If you have made arrangements to buy a pup from a breeder, you can ask her precisely what you should have. She will be flattered and delighted that you care to ask. Otherwise, the bare essentials are a toy, two bowls, a bag of good-quality puppy food, and a nylon or leather collar and leash. Soon enough you'll be putting a larger smile on the pet store owner's face.

What should I eventually buy?

Most new dog owners have no idea of the wide range of combs, brushes, leashes, and collars that exist for their selection. Because various breeds have particular requirements, it is best to wait for most purchases until you have discussed them with the breeder or an expert who can give you the benefit of his experience. Collars can be chain, leather, or nylon; narrow or wide; flat buckle or slip style. Leashes may be nylon web, rolled nylon, $\frac{1}{4}$- to 1-inch leather, or combination "show leads" with the collar attached. Do not buy the chain leash so prominently displayed in stores; chain bruises your hands.

Plastic, ceramic, or metal dog bowls may be purchased to suit the tiniest Chihuahua to the largest Saint Bernard appetite. Metal bowls have greatest longevity, particularly for large, active dogs who like to play catch with them.

A crate to fit your pup as he grows to maturity should be your next purchase. You'll have a choice between wire mesh and hard-shell plastic, which is the type airlines require.

In addition to all of this, you'll soon make decisions about shampoos; a heartworm preventive; fences or runs; nail clippers, scissors, grinders, or files; bristle or pin brushes in all sizes and shapes; fine-, medium-, or large-toothed combs; and the all-important item, a pooper-scooper! You may also need hair clippers, a puppy gate, grooming spray, training equipment, ear and teeth cleaner, flea spray or an equivalent, and a tack box to store all of your equipment. Toys of all sizes and shapes please any dog.

The smile on the pet supplier's face becomes larger along with your total bill.

Please suggest some unusual gifts for Shag on special occasions? What can I buy for some of my dog-loving friends?

Specialty catalogues for canine items abound. If you send for a couple of them or enter Shag in a show, you will soon be on mailing lists. These catalogues are advertised in dog magazines.

In them you can find a potpourri of necessities and just-for-fun items: fancy dog beds, chew bones, sleeping bags, specialized leashes and training equipment, a year's supply of dog biscuits, and extravagant dog outfits from raincoats and boots to sailor suits and tuxedos. For owners, you'll find personalized business cards and Christmas cards for kennels; breed-decorated ties, clothing, statues, cups, jewelry, books, notepaper, belt buckles, and mailbox ornaments; and magazine subscriptions for all tastes and breeds. Other thoughtful ideas are gift certificates for boarding or for show weekends, as well as customized sketches and paintings of their dogs and many, many more possibilities.

PART TWO

RAISING YOUR DOG RIGHT

6

Puddle Problems

How long does it take to housebreak a puppy or an adult that has been raised outside? I've heard it's harder to train a male; is that true?

House training a puppy is very much like potty training a toddler. It depends on how diligent *you* are. First thing in the morning, take your puppy outdoors. As soon as he hears you stir, he'll be up ready for fun; this stimulates natural urges. Take him out when he wakes from naps, after you arrive home from an absence, before playtime, and after meals. When he performs in the right spot, show your pleasure with plenty of praise and pats. His control will soon improve, and you will be able to decrease the frequency of his outings. Trained properly and patiently, young dogs can be quite dependable by three months of age. Usually, an adult can be trained quickly, once you learn his habits and adjust him to your schedule. Until you are certain of your dog, puppy or adult, confine him to an uncarpeted area that can be easily cleaned if an accident occurs.

Males tend to be dominant; thus, by instinct, they mark their territory. This habit can cause some problems at puberty or after being used at stud. If this occurs, reinforce your housebreaking training and remain alert for catalysts, for example, when another dog enters your home.

Should I paper-train first?

Two situations may make paper training more convenient: if you live in a twentieth-floor apartment or if you are away from home all day. Otherwise, there is no need, and this only causes you to train twice.

If you decide to paper-train, confine your pet to a small area or room. Cover part of the floor with several layers of newspaper. When it is soiled, strip off and dispose of the top layers, leaving only the very bottom paper. This emits a slight scent noticeable only to the dog and encourages her to return to the same spot. Gradually decrease the area covered by papers until your dog is completely dependable.

Should I hit Bandit with a newspaper when he goofs, or rub his nose in it?

Bandit is not leaving puddles and piles to irritate you. If you hit him, he will learn to cringe when you approach, and if you rub his nose in his mistake, you will have twice the cleaning up to do—the dog *and* the floor.

Be alert and try to catch Bandit with his pants down (so to speak). Show vocal disapproval: a loud *Noooo*!!! Immediately pick up Bandit or snap on his leash and take him outdoors. With any luck, he may be able to squeeze out a drop or two in the right place. Now you can follow up with a "*Goooooooood* boy!" and a pat on the head. Until Bandit aces the course, never walk around in your bare feet with the lights off.

Suddenly my dog is breaking training. What can I do?

First take your pet to the veterinarian. Some physical problems, such as a bladder infection, can cause accidents. If no medical reason is evident, give her a social checkup. Have her life and routine been altered? Have you moved or changed her feeding time, or is she under stress? Look for differences in your own life-style—have you recently married or divorced? Or are you just working overtime? Even though she may control herself all day while you're home, she may feel neglected if you're gone for eight hours.

Try to spend some extra, high-quality time with your pet. If you can't find a reason or alleviate a problem, revert to puppy-time training.

My old dog Max has lost some control but feels good otherwise. How should I handle this?

Your veterinarian may be able to administer medication that may help or give you some advice on changing Max's diet or adjusting his feeding schedule. You can also try confining Max to an area that is easy to clean or even resort to diapers. This problem is difficult for both you and the dog. Max is ashamed and most owners are dismayed, upset because of the mess and because an old friend is having debilitating symptoms. Increase his outings and try to remain understanding. Punishment will not make him or his bladder young again.

What can I use to clean up a mess?

Use paper towels to soak up moisture. Scrub the carpet with a stain remover, such as Sop Up. A solution mixing equal amounts of white vinegar and hot water helps neutralize odor.

Why does my Buffy piddle when I pet her?

Wild dogs show their submission to dominant members of the pack by lowering their heads, lying on their backs with groin exposed, and by urinating. Buffy feels your dominance and, in effect, is saying, "I know you're the boss. Please don't hurt me." Unfortunately, this irritates the owner and the act is usually followed by a sign of more dominance: yelling or hitting.

Try to figure out the source of her submission. Perhaps you have been wielding too firm a hand and you need to relax a bit in your relationship with Buffy. Ease up on continual corrections. Or it may simply be that Buffy is timid; attempt to build her confidence and change your manner when greeting her. Lower yourself to her level by sitting, kneeling, or even lying on the floor. Call her to you, but don't reach for her. Let her make the overtures. Talk to her in a gentle voice, telling her what a good girl she is. If she continues her submissive urination, rise and walk away. Do this as many times as necessary until she realizes she is not the focus of your entire world. Don't coo to her, reinforcing her behavior, but also do not try to correct it at this point. She can do nothing to control the action; it is involuntary.

How do you train a dog to go to one area? I've heard they will, but Johnny goes to forty-five places. It sure would be easier for cleanup.

Dogs are creatures of habit and like a life of routine. This is why they react well to repetitive training methods.

As soon as you buy your dog, start taking him to the same spot for his outing. Leave one of Johnny's "successes" as a calling card for him. Remain alert and ready to head him to his toilet area immediately. Scoop him up, saying "No!"; move to the right place quickly; plant him and say, "OK!" Or walk him on leash to the same area each time to acclimate him to the proper place and to relieving himself when attached to a lead. This is a convenience for trips.

Be prepared to wait him out. When action commences, sing his praises, and soon he'll be "Johnny-on-the-spot."

Some small dogs can actually be trained to a litter box, a convenience for owners who are gone all day or who live in skyscraper apartments.

Why do breeders suggest crate training?

From about eight weeks of age, most dogs prefer not to mess their sleeping area. In fact, many start even earlier. Breeders often separate the litter's living quarters from the toilet area by placing a blanket or carpet in the "bedroom" and papers in the "bathroom." They say that even three-week-old puppies toddle from their living quarters to the papers.

As pups are sold, new owners can take advantage of this inborn cleanliness to facilitate housebreaking with the utilization of a crate. Within reason, your pup will hold herself for a longer length of time when confined to her "den." The person who is gone all day can try the following method: the pup should be fed early in the morning, taken out, then allowed to play while her owner is dressing. Take her out one more time, then tell her "crate" or "bed" and pop her inside. Until the pup is about four months old, try to make arrangements to have her fed and exercised again at noon. Many young dogs train in an amazingly short time.

Crates are the most marvelous invention for dog owners since dogs!

I've heard dogs are clean creatures, but Sally's a pig. Is she backward?

Perhaps in her social amenities! Puppies raised by conscientious breeders who keep the whelping area clean and disinfected usually grow to be fastidious adults. Occasionally, unavoidable circumstances occur. Dogs raised in kennels or plagued by diarrhea are difficult to keep completely clean, no matter how hard their owners try. Rarely, a dog is just a slob. Try to remain one step ahead of Sally. Pick up her feed bowl within fifteen minutes, so she can't dump it. Offer her water several times a day rather than leaving out a bowl for her to dive into. Make frequent pickup forays.

Some dogs, like some kids, simply seem drawn to dirt and bad-smelling things.

I'm embarrassed to say this to anyone, but my dog has started relieving himself on my bed. Why and what can I do?

Unless your dog has a kidney problem or bladder infection, this behavior is definitely a stress reaction or a protest. When the owner suddenly is away for longer periods of time a dog may use this means as a bid for attention. This also occurs when someone else moves into the bedroom and usurps the dog's position in his master's heart. Perhaps he feels he "don't get no respect."

If your veterinarian has ruled out any physical cause, pay more attention to your dog. Take him out to walk or to play fetch. Try to avoid such a situation by introducing subtle changes into the normal routine. For instance, if you are engaged, ask your fiancé to help with a doggy chore and to play with your pet while you're busy elsewhere. If sleeping quarters are to be altered, move your dog out of the bedroom before your new roomie moves in. If you try to solve this problem by simply locking your bedroom door, he may transfer his resentment to your favorite chair.

My dog has long hair, and when her stools are soft, it's a mess. Any suggestions?

Keep the hair clipped around the genitals and the anus. Even dogs whose Standards specify a natural look are often trimmed for hygienic purposes. Never permit any residue of droppings to remain on her coat, as it invites parasites and irritates the skin, as well as being unsightly and smelling unpleasant.

When traveling, take her usual food and containers of water along, because changes often upset the digestive system. If you must make a change, make the adjustment slowly, mixing in her usual diet and water with the new. Additionally, be careful to keep her menu simple and easily digestible—no beer and pizza allowed.

7

Lookin' Good!

How often should I brush Bobby?

Grooming frequency depends on the length and texture of your dog's coat. If Bobby is a Lhasa Apso or Old English Sheepdog with long, thick hair that tends to mat, a thorough brushing once a day is ideal. Long, harsh hair such as that found on Collies stays healthy and shining with a skin-deep grooming session once a week and a daily touch-up. Medium or short lengths such as the coats of Cardigan Corgis or Border Terriers can be kept spiffy with a vigorous weekly brushing. Mist the coat with a grooming spray or plain water to ease the task and to avoid breakage of hair.

Should I bathe my long-haired dog before I groom her? How often should my dog be bathed? What about a conditioner?

Unless your dog is extremely filthy, brush and comb her first before you bathe her. Shampooing can set mats and make her coat even more difficult to detangle.

Dogs do not perspire as we do, so frequent bathing is not necessary. In fact, such a regime would wash away the natural oils that cause dogs' coats to shine and limit broken hair. A spring and fall bath during shedding season is advisable for pets. Many are bathed more or less often, however, without adverse effects. In fact, some show dogs are bathed every week or two using gentle shampoos and conditioners.

Be careful to pick the proper shampoo. Talk to a groomer, handler, or your pup's breeder and ask for suggestions. Some breeds require a shampoo made espccially for harsh coats; others need one that is suited for fine, silky hair. Shampoos for black, white, apricot, or brown tones enhance coat color. Equal caution must be taken in choosing conditioners, particularly if you intend to show your dog. These products may simply be mat detanglers or may soften a coat that is supposed to be harsh.

I like the look of long-haired dogs, but I'm afraid I won't have the time to keep up with the care.

Good grooming for long-coated dogs does require time. The frequency of care is such that it precludes regular professional grooming for most owners. If you can't manage weekly brushing, somebody must, or your pet suffers discomfort as well as being unattractive. Before you buy a dog, ascertain how much grooming your breed choice needs and determine who is willing to act as Phydeaux's hairdresser.

From the time you bring your ball of fluff home, set up a schedule and try to stick to it, for instance, "I will brush Phydeaux every Thursday (or every night, if need be) during the evening news." If you carry out your resolution, Phydeaux's coat will be a credit to him and to you.

Grooming sessions can become a battle or a therapeutic social event. Begin with several short periods, gradually decreasing the frequency and increasing the length of time. Maintain control of your pup from the start and make him behave during grooming. It is only natural your pup won't want to stop playing and bouncing to submit to your dull ideas of spending time. Talk to him while you're brushing and combing; tell him he's soooo beautiful and a good puppy when he stands still for even a moment. Take advantage of this interval for a bit of training: while grooming, the owner can teach a dog "Sit," "Stand," "Down," and "Stay."

This is also a good time to conduct a checkup; look for possible parasites, infections, wounds, or lumps. By the time Phydeaux is an old dog, you and he will welcome this one-on-one attention.

What kind of brush or comb should I use? Should I spray anything onto his coat while grooming?

Again, this depends on the coat. Combs with wooden or metal handles and fine, medium, or coarse teeth may be chosen. Pin, bristle, or slicker brushes are sold in a variety of shapes and sizes.

In addition, several other grooming tools such as rakes, strippers, shedding blades, and grooming gloves are useful, if you know what you're doing. Don't be afraid to ask questions of experts. Even if your pet is professionally beautified, the groomer would rather work with a clean, unmatted coat than with one that looks like a tumbleweed. The well-kept dog also costs less to groom, because it requires less time to clip or brush.

I'm going crazy trying to keep ahead of the mats on my one-year-old pup. It wasn't this bad before. Why is this happening now?

Some time between ten and fourteen months, the "big shed" occurs. As the puppy coat is lost, it becomes entangled in the new hair, and lalapalooza mats are formed. Increase your grooming sessions to twice a week or even more often; check daily for mats by running your fingers through her tresses. After two or three weeks, her hair will be scanty until her adult coat comes into full bloom.

Use one of the products noted for removing tangles. Follow directions for diluting and spray the mat thoroughly, working the lotion through to the ends with your fingers. Then use a grooming rake or mat splitter to remove the tangle. Holding the knot of hair next to the body, gently pull the teeth of the tool through the mass several times with a picking action.

What breeds need professional grooming? Can I learn to do this?

Courses and books offer tips and training for grooming all breeds, and some people enjoy being amateur hairdressers. Most pet owners elect to have a professional do the job for them, however, for it is time-

consuming. Tools are expensive, and finesse comes only with a great amount of experience.

Therefore, most Schnauzers, Poodles, Cockers, Wheaten Terriers, Bichon Frises, and Bedlingtons are trimmed by pros. Owners of broken-coated terriers often find it easier to let a groomer pluck, strip, or trim their fuzzy friends. Many people who have breeds with thick, long coats (Lhasas, Old English, Pekingese, and Shih Tzus) make monthly appointments to have their pets groomed at a canine beauty parlor. These dogs can be kept beautifully coiffed with just a surface brushing and diligent dematting at home. Even those dogs that require only a "lick and a promise" can benefit by an occasional visit to a pro for a spring cleaning.

Can I trim or shave down a long-haired dog? Marcy's old and arthritic, and I'm not much better. It would be easier for both of us.

Unless you are currently showing Marcy, there's no reason why you cannot ease grooming for both of you. Pets or retired show dogs may be clipped in whatever style the owner prefers.

Some breed Standards specify no trimming or alterations of coats on dogs being shown in the conformation rings. Many owners do trim around the genital and anal areas, however, for hygienic purposes.

Do not clip Marcy in an erroneous attempt at air-conditioning during summer heat. The long hair actually acts as an insulation that keeps her cool and prevents her being painfully sunburned. (Yes, they can!)

Should I clip the whiskers or not? What trimming is involved in most breeds?

Trimming whiskers has become a controversial issue. Many of the smooth-faced breeds' vibrissae are snipped off to heighten the sleek look of the dog. Some people now feel this is ill advised because the whiskers act as sensory feelers.

Handlers of some terriers, setters, and spaniels trim coats to neaten outlines and to draw attention to specific attributes. Winning ribbons is impossible without learning this art. The technique calls for experience and expertise and should be learned from someone adept at the procedure.

Gizmo's coat is soft, and the Standard says its supposed to be harsh. Any suggestions?

First, be sure the shampoo you're using is for harsh coats. Shampoo several days in advance of a show, allowing time for the natural oils to replenish themselves. Using a chalk powder to match Gizmo's coloring gives the coat a harsher feel. Coat texturizer also helps for a short time. Of course, show rules specify that such products must be brushed out before entering the ring, so the effects are temporary. Bathing or trimming with a clipper softens the coat. Harsh-coated show terriers such as Scotties or Cairns should be hand-plucked and rarely, if ever, bathed.

The opposite effect, softening coats, can be easily accomplished by cream rinses and conditioners.

My dog is white, but she gets so dirty. How can I clean her up?

White areas on a dog's coat often yellow from eating, drinking water, chewing on a bone, or playing in the backyard—normal doggy activities. Bluing shampoo helps to make an off-white dog sparkling white again. Exhibitors often have formulas and mixtures to put on white areas after shampooing, eliminating the "ring around the collar" annoyance. Suds with one of these products or mixtures, then rub in a chalk/cornstarch blend, dry, and brush out the excess. This procedure lasts long enough for your dog to impress your guests at a party or to run around the show ring a few times.

Stains caused by teary eyes can be a problem with some breeds. Boric acid powder and commercial products are of some help.

Prevention is the best policy. Use a dryer rather than air drying, attack stains immediately, and don't feed your Samoyed spaghetti sauce. Do remember dogs will be dogs, however, and—like their young two-legged pals—are attracted to mud puddles and other enticements.

Is there anything that can prevent Kaz from losing his coat? When will he shed?

Seasonal shedding of hair in spring and fall is a fact of life when you have dogs. Females sometimes shed according to their heat cycles.

Regular, vigorous brushing stimulates new hair growth and removes much of the dead coat as it is lost. Show dogs are occasionally kept in air-conditioned premises to fend off Mother Nature for a short time. Eventually, however, even the best efforts yield to a superior force, and one day you will find most of Kaz's coat on the floor instead of on him. Hair loss can be sped by warm baths if you wish to hasten the inevitable. Remember, it *will* grow back!

Which dogs don't shed? Do shorthaired dogs shed less than those with long hair?

Only hairless dogs don't shed at all (see p. 27). Short-coated dogs shed as profusely as their relatives with longer coats. The hair's just shorter.

The dead hair of some breeds is shed mostly into their own coats. When it is brushed out, hair won't cover your furniture and clothing or waft around the air. Schnauzers, Poodles, Pulik, Komondor, and Soft-Coated Wheaten Terriers all offer this advantage.

How do I cut Corky's toenails, and how often should it be done? What if I make them bleed?

A groomer, breeder, or veterinarian can demonstrate the proper way to cut toenails. Although trimming nails is usually a chore neither you nor Corky relishes, it must be done for health purposes. Nails continue growing throughout the dog's life and, if unclipped, will spread the toes. They may even deform her foot or curl under to pierce it.

Begin trimming from the time you bring your puppy home to acquaint yourself with the growth of the quick and to acclimate your dog to a lifetime necessity. Cutting nails is like paying taxes: not much fun, but necessary and—done right—merely distasteful but painless.

You may choose a dog nail clipper or scissors, grinder or file, whatever you are most comfortable with. Lay the dog down and look for the quick, which runs through the middle. This bloodline is easier to see in white nails. Clip a small amount at a time, particularly with black ones, until the quick is visible. Should you nip the quick, stop the blood with styptic powder.

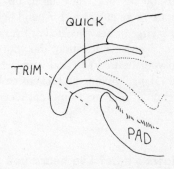

Frequency of clipping depends on heredity, the shape of your dog's foot, the flooring she is on most of the time, and the amount of exercise Corky receives. Some dogs that run on cement keep the nails worn down themselves. Others, in carpeted homes with limited outings, must be trimmed weekly. On the average, a dog's nails need to be trimmed about every two weeks. Don't forget the dewclaws, located on the inside of the legs.

How can I tell whether Lad has fleas, and what do I use to get rid of them? How do I remove ticks?

Fleas cause severe itching, worse than that caused by mosquito bites. Flea bites send allergic dogs into frenzies. If Lad is frantically scratching, look for signs of parasites at the root of the tail and on the belly.

Kill a tick by spraying or dipping the dog with an insecticide. After a moment, it will loosen its hold, and you will be able to grasp it near the head, pull firmly, and remove it. Disinfect the site and your hands to wash away toxic substances.

Prevention is the best method of protecting Lad from being "bugged." As pest season approaches, check him frequently for evidence of parasites, even if he isn't itching, especially after walks in the woods. Spray or powder your dog at the first sign of a flea; the pill, Proban, and the external preventive, Pro-Spot, are also effective. Spray *all* pets, cats and dogs, indoor and outdoor animals to break the "sharing" cycle. Don't forget to spray his premises on a routine basis, every week or two, because fleas lay their eggs *off* the dog.

If you're too late and the bugs have taken up residence, use a shampoo or dip. Dips are more effective. Flea and tick collars may be useful, but if your dog is large or heavy-coated or lives outdoors, collars will not do the job. For a severe infestation, dip your pets and release residual flea bombs in your house. You and your pets must leave the premises during the "bombing." Follow instructions exactly. This should be followed with a regime of spraying to prevent reoccurrences.

How can I clean Hawk's ears? I've heard you're supposed to pluck inside the ears of long-haired dogs. How do you do that?

Moisten a cloth or cotton ball with mineral oil and rub the inside of the ear, removing excess wax and dirt. A product such as Eargard can keep ears clean if you squeeze a drop or two into them during the weekly grooming session. Rub the base of the ear to spread the solution.

For health purposes, dogs with profuse hair such as Poodles and Schnauzers *must* have the inside of their ears plucked. Rub the ear canal with mineral oil or sprinkle with an antibiotic ear powder, grasp a few strands with tweezers or your fingers, and pull it out. Veterinarians and groomers can perform this chore if you wish.

Should I pluck around his eyes, so he can see better?

Pet owners may prefer to clip the excess hair above the dog's eyes. Unless you trim his face every week or two, bristly new growth below the eyes may irritate them. It may be better to comb and train the hair to fall to the sides. Show dog groomers should check the breed Standard before making any alterations in the coat.

Help! My dog ran into a skunk. What do I do besides boarding him in the next county?

Believe it or not, the best solution for this smelly problem is dousing the dog with Massengill douche, which has a neutralizing effect on the odor. It's certainly less messy and more effective than tomato juice, which is also helpful.

What are ear mites?

Both cats and dogs are susceptible to ear mites and indiscriminately pass them to one another. These eight-legged parasites live only in the ear and chew on the ear canal lining (ouch!) for their meals. Intense irritation results, with an accumulation of brown-black wax. Mites must be identified by a veterinarian and treated with specific medication. Owners must be sure to continue the dosage for the full time prescribed. This is necessary to eradicate the mites hatched from eggs after the adults are destroyed.

My vet says my dog has walking dandruff. What on earth is that?

"Walking dandruff," or dandruff mites, are parasites that occasionally plague dogs, causing mild itching and white flaking. They are easily eliminated by use of an insecticide dip.

8
Weighing In

When will Callie stop growing?

Most dogs grow to their full height at the time of adolescence (about one year). Their bodies continue to deepen, broaden, and develop musculature until the age of two or three. Of course, this is only an average for medium-size breeds; miniatures reach physical maturity more quickly, and giants may still be filling out at four. The larger the breed, the longer the dog takes to reach its peak.

Do big feet mean Godzilla is going to grow up to be a big dog?

All puppies seem to have feet and ears three sizes too big for the rest of them. It's part of their puppy charm. Eventually they do grow into these features; although feet are a sign of ultimate size, they are not as good an indication as bone. Is Godzilla big- or small-boned? Size is relative: even the most oversized Pug's foot is smaller than the littlest Akita's paw.

What are the largest and smallest breeds?

The smallest breed, according to its Standard requirements, is the Chihuahua. Some Poodles and Yorkies are very tiny too. The tiniest dog on record is a Yorkshire Terrier named Sylvia, with an adult weight of ten ounces.

Leaving the postage-scale pups, the Saint Bernards weigh in at the truck scale. Officially, the heaviest dog listed in the *Guinness Book of World Records 1985 Special Edition* is a Saint, "Benedictine," at a mammoth 305 pounds.

The tallest are the Great Dane and the Irish Wolfhound, with a Dane named Shamgret Danzas measuring a tree-topping 41½ inches!

Is the runt of the litter a bad choice?

If a runt survives infancy, it can be an excellent choice as a pet. A large litter, positioning in the womb, and matings spread over several days can all cause a variation in the size of newborns. Of course, physical abnormalities, particularly those affecting the heart or digestive system, can also cause a puny pup.

If all is well physically, the smallest pup also must be sturdy and strong-willed to survive. To obtain equal time at the chow line, she must be able to ward off her biggest siblings' attempts at usurping her place. A little intervention by the breeder, ensuring that the littlest has first dibs and reserved seating, helps.

Pups gain and grow at amazing rates in the nursery, and many times the smallest catches up to most of the others. In fact, each week's weigh-in may show a different leader or straggler. By the time the pups are one year, the "runt" may well be the biggest.

Does my puppy need vitamin supplements?

Follow your breeder's and veterinarian's advice. Although good-quality foods supply necessary nutrients, specific cases may require the use of supplements.

I like big, and I want to make sure my next dog is a whopper. Is there anything wrong with that?

Of course not, big dogs need homes too. Some breeds have problems if a dog becomes larger than recommended, however. Perhaps the breed creators found that agility decreased or bone diseases increased in oversize animals. So look for one of the breeds that is *supposed* to be king-size.

Still, size isn't the most important characteristic in a pet, and other attributes should be considered. Would you hire a new employee just because of her height? You'd probably consider such factors as personality, neatness, intelligence, and work ability over size, unless you're a basketball team manager. Even then, you may prefer a six-foot sureshot to an eight-foot klutz.

Will feeding more make Spot larger?

Yes, it'll make him larger, but not taller. Remember, you're not fattening up your dog for market. You want Spot to be healthy, and the best way to ensure that is to keep him in prime condition, neither too heavy nor too thin. Skimping on quantity or quality definitely can produce an undersize dog, but overfeeding will only increase fat rather than Spot's size and shorten his life span.

Why do dogs grow in such awkward ways? Kim is nine months and looks like a freak! Her rear's higher than her front!

Just like teenagers, adolescent dogs grow in spurts, with one part of the body shooting ahead of the others. Young boys sometimes seem to be all feet, nose, and Adam's apple. As Kim reaches puberty, her rear legs may grow faster than the front ones, or her body seem to lengthen into a freight train. At the same time, she loses her puppy coat, and she looks like one of Dickens's scraggly orphans.

Just continue loving her and keep the faith. Remember the ugly duckling. One day Kim will regain her puppyhood promise of beauty.

My vet told me the lower jaw often grows later than the upper. Is that true?

This is why some pups that have a perfect occlusion at eight weeks have underbites by eight months. Occasionally, this problem corrects again a month or two later when the upper jaw catches up. Some show breeders actually prefer that a young pup have a small overbite so that it has a head start when the lower jaw starts to grow.

The bite usually doesn't matter to buyers looking only for a companion. They're only interested in whether or not he will bite, not in his under-, over-, or crooked bite. Nevertheless, if you intend to show, you should discuss this matter with the breeder. Ask whether the breed or his lines have problems and, if so, what type of mouth you should look for as you choose your pup. He won't want you to be disappointed or to select a dog that won't win in the show ring because his bite is off.

Chewing on bones exercises the lower jaw and is sometimes thought to aid in improving overbites. Some owners also apply pressure on the jaw that needs to grow, by putting their thumbs on the inside and pulling forward. Whether or not these techniques are successful, they do not change the dog's genetic makeup, and his progeny are also likely to have problem bites.

All the other six-month-old dogs look so much bigger than Rex. Is there something wrong with him?

Do you remember your own youth? One of the boys thought he'd never grow, and one of the girls was taller than everyone else, including the teachers. The others were in between, but hardly anyone matched the doctor's charts. If it will make you feel better, have Rex examined, but most likely he's just a late bloomer. Physical diseases that stunt growth usually produce other symptoms as well.

In some breeds, smaller is better. Which are they?

Most breed Standards state a minimum size as well as a maximum, because deformities can occur when dogs become too small. Nevertheless, the Affenpinscher, Chihuahua, Italian Greyhound, and Japanese Chin give preference to smaller specimens. In fact, it is common for females of many Toy breeds to be bigger than the males because the bitches need to be large enough to carry and whelp a litter normally.

What breeds have disqualifications on size? What is considered too small or too big?

Breeds with size disqualifications are measured in the ring by a U-shaped instrument called a *wicket*. The wicket is grasped at the curve and passed over the top of the dog's shoulders (withers). A straight bar across the U measures the correct height.

Most breeds allow an inch over or under the ideal height. Golden Retrievers, Brittanys, Cockers, Vizslas, Weimaraners, Bassets, Beagles, Whippets, Akitas, Belgian Malinois and Sheepdogs, Great Danes, Shelties, Siberians, Schnauzers, Miniature Pinschers, Papillons, and Poodles all have height disqualifications in their Standards and may be measured in the ring.

My mutt's head looks too big for her body. Why?

As explained in previous chapters, knowledge of breeds and purebred lines enables a breeder to plan a litter of proportionate pups. When Maw Mastiff and Paw Pomeranian are the only ones involved in the planning, weird things occur. Some of the pups may have the Mastiff body with the Pom coat, the dam's size with the sire's physical features, or the Pom's body with the Mastiff's head.

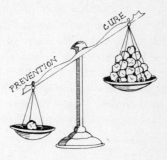

9

An Ounce of Prevention

How do I choose a veterinarian?

As with any occupation—plumbers, lawyers, baseball players, or veterinarians—there are great ones and the not-so-greats. Talk to professional breeders for suggestions. They often have more of an investment in their animals, which must be protected with the best medical attention possible. In addition, because breeders have more dogs, they spend more time at clinics! They know which vets are specialists in various fields and are easiest to talk to.

Take your dog to a clinic for a physical exam and make your own checkup while you're there. Is the staff friendly and caring? Are the premises clean, and is modern equipment available? Find out whether X rays and blood tests are performed on the premises and what other services are offered. Ask the veterinarian whether he or she or others on the staff have a specialty or areas of expertise. Are they available for emergencies after hours, or are they associated with an emergency clinic?

During the first few visits, you can note additional significant facts. Is there a rapport among you, the vet, and your dog? Does the doctor trust your intuition? He or she should keep abreast of new methods, techniques, diagnoses, and other medical advances. The vet should be willing to explain your dog's health and treatment in lay terms, not overwhelming you with fifty-dollar medical words.

Once you have discovered this sterling character, keep up your end of the relationship by following her advice. Maintain a medical record on each dog you own and keep up-to-date on regular preventive care and vaccinations. Be aware of your pet's normal routine. If you are tuned into your dog's physical habits and his attitude, you will receive bad vibes when he is feeling off-key. Notice whether he is listless or hyperactive or drinking too much water. Parents notice when their child has a "funny" look in her eyes or is too quiet. Keep alert for those same symptoms in your pet so you can warn *his* doctor.

What is a dog's normal temperature? How do I take it?

A dog's temperature is 101.5 degrees, with 100 to 102.5 within normal range. To take the temperature, obtain a rectal thermometer (one used for babies will do), shake it down several degrees, and dip the end in petroleum jelly. Insert the thermometer about one inch into the rectum and wait about two minutes. The temperature of newborns is 96 to 100 degrees; this is one reason it is important to keep neonatal puppies warm.

Taking the temperature can help *you* determine whether there is a problem, and reporting the temperature to the vet gives *him* a head start in making a diagnosis.

What shots are necessary? When does Shadow need "permanent" shots?

Veterinarians suggest inoculating your dog against distemper, hepatitis (adenovirus), parainfluenza, parvovirus, and coronavirus. *Leptospira* and *Bordetella* vaccines are also available. In addition, most states require immunization against rabies.

No shots are permanent. After the barrage of inoculations during puppyhood, Shadow's shots must be boostered annually, although some states allow a three-year rabies vaccine. Even house pets who "never go anywhere" can catch airborne viruses and "bugs" clinging to your clothing or shoes. Conscientious owners want to protect their pets in every possible way. Prevention is easier, less expensive, and less agonizing than trying to cure one of these dread diseases.

Don't forget, not only is Shadow your best friend, you are his best friend, and it's up to you to protect him. Unless he's unusually talented, he can't drive himself to the vet for care!

How do I give Oly pills and liquid medicine?

Taking medicine is not a free choice, so occasionally owners must coax their dogs to cooperate. To give pills, place your left hand on top of Oly's muzzle with the thumb on one side and fingers on the other. Exert pressure in and up, opening his mouth. The lips will be curved over the upper teeth, so closing his mouth will hurt him more than you.

Take the pill with your other hand, place it over the back of the tongue, and close the mouth—removing your hand first, of course! Tip Oly's head back slightly, stroking his throat with your hand to induce swallowing. When his tongue appears, it indicates he has swallowed, although some manage to tuck the pill in a corner and spit it back at you. For such a picky pooch, coat the pills with mineral or vegetable oil, allowing them to slide easily down the throat, or squirt some water in after the pill to force Oly to swallow. Another method is to place the medication in a ball of ground beef, liverwurst, or any favorite snack. Crushing the medication makes it easier to disguise. Offer a plain tidbit, followed by the medicated piece, and another of the "real McCoy" quickly. He'll be so busy swallowing all the goodies, he'll miss your trick.

There's one more method that rarely fails: crush the medicine and mix it into the old stick-to-the-mouth peanut butter. Occasionally, we still manage to outsmart our dogs!

For liquids, tip Oly's head back and lift his lip, pouring in the medication. It will even run between clenched teeth and down the throat. Liquids also can be administered via an eyedropper or syringe (without the needle). This is so simple that you may wish to talk to the vet about whether the pills can be crushed and mixed with water.

When should I take a stool sample to the vet?

All puppies should be tested for worms by the breeder and again by the new owner. Dogs can easily reinfest themselves, particularly when they are still part of a litter. No matter how fastidious a breeder is, puppies "litter" too much and too often to keep their living area 100 percent clean. Dogs are most often infested by stool contamination, but fleas, rodents, and even the dam can pass parasites along. If your dog eats uncooked meat, including rabbits or other wild animals, she can ingest the culprits.

It's a good idea to test adult dogs for worms during their annual physical and before bitches are bred. A mild infestation may not cause symptoms, but weight loss, change of appetite, a dull hair coat, or a loose and/or bloody stool may indicate worms. Segments of worms also may be vomited or passed in the stool.

P.S. Just take a small sample (about a teaspoonful) to the vet. A bucketful isn't necessary!

What kind of worms can he get?

Hookworms, tapeworms, roundworms, and whipworms infest dogs' intestinal tracts. It is important to know which worm is present in order to eradicate the pests properly. Don't depend on over-the-counter "all-purpose" wormers. No one product eliminates all, and the wrong dosage can kill your pet, as can heavy infestations of parasites. Some worms must be evicted more than once before these freeloaders leave their place of residence. Once your dog has been wormed, purify his toilet area with the strongest possible disinfectant.

The heartworm and the rare lungworm, which clog these vital organs, require specialized tests and specific medication.

I know about fleas and ticks. What other kinds of external parasites may attack my dog?

Other pests your dog may encounter are lice and a variety of parasitic mites. Mite infestation, often called "mange," includes poultry, dandruff, sarcoptic, and demodectic forms. Although dog lice *do not* transfer to humans, some forms of mange do. They all can cause intense itching and irritation with secondary infections. Because treatments are specific, a diagnosis must be made by your vet. Fortunately, once identified, most are easily eliminated.

Mosquitoes and flies are annoying to dogs, especially those who live outdoors. Use a preventive salve on erect ears, which seem especially attractive to flies. Plant marigolds around the kennel to repel insects, and spray the area with insecticide, carefully following label instructions.

When Whiskey scoots on his behind, does it mean he has worms?

One pest that does not plague dogs is the pinworm, which can cause anal itching in humans. Thus, "scooting" commonly indicates the dog's anal glands are full. These glands should empty spontaneously during defecation; if they don't, the swelling and pressure cause irritation and pain. The dog attempts to alleviate this by rubbing his rear on the ground, peering inquisitively at his behind, or jumping up suddenly as though he'd been bitten.

Your vet can quickly empty Whiskey's impacted anal glands to give him relief. Left untreated, the glands can abscess and rupture into putrid, draining tracts.

How do I get a urine specimen from Flossie?

Put your dog on leash and follow her with an aluminum pie pan. Although you must be on your toes, ready to dart in in "midstream" with your container, you only need a small amount. It's easier to capture a male's sample, because he stops at every tree and post!

Should I crop my Boxer or not? That seems cruel!

Americans and much of the world are accustomed to seeing certain breeds—Boxers, Schnauzers, Great Danes, Bouviers, Briards, Brussels Griffons, Affenpinschers, Doberman and Miniature Pinschers, Standard Manchester and American Staffordshire Terriers—with ears made to stand by surgical trimming. In England, ear cropping has been outlawed for many years, and a few other countries are following suit. Natural ears are being seen more often.

Nevertheless, many people still prefer the look of the erect ear, and cropping remains a common cosmetic surgery. This bid for canine beauty may be compared to a person's having a face-lift or a nose job. If the surgery is done at a very early age, success is greater and discomfort is minimized. Be sure you choose a vet familiar with the procedure in your particular breed, because fashions differ and styles change over the years.

What about docking and dewclaws?

Cropping ears, docking tails, and removing dewclaws were originally performed to prevent injuries of working dogs. Docking and dewclaw removal ideally should be performed at two days of age when the wounds are easily healed and quickly forgotten.

How long does a dog take to recover from surgery, and what special care will my dog need?

The type of surgery and whatever complications develop, if any, will dictate what the recovery period is. Animals seem to bounce back more quickly from surgery than humans do. In fact, the major problem often is keeping your pet less active for a few days. A crate helps if he tries to overdo.

Because bandages are rarely put on dogs, the wound area should be kept clean. Watch for seepage or swelling at the incision site. An important nursing duty is watching for signs of infection. The temperature should be taken for several days after any major internal surgery. Follow veterinary instructions and return for postsurgical examinations. Stitches are usually removed in one to two weeks.

Make sure your dog drinks plenty of cold, clean water. Don't rush into feeding huge meals in an attempt to put him back on his feet. It's often a good idea to skip the first day's feeding, giving a small amount the day after surgery. "Doctor" his food by saturating it with chicken broth, if you wish, making it more appealing to the patient.

Ferdinand likes to eat flowers. Is that okay?

Dogs will be dogs, and a plant bulb can look as inviting to chew on as a ball. The leaves, root, bulb, flower, seeds, and bark of some seemingly innocuous plants can cause anything from a mild gastric upset to a fatal poisoning. See Plants Poisonous to Dogs (pp. 183–84) for dangerous flora.

Antifreeze also seems to be particularly yummy, but extremely poisonous to pets. Household cleaning products can be a threat as well. Specific antidotes exist for some poisons, but many have none. Even

chocolate in large quantities can prove fatal. Therefore, dogproof your house, so your pet is safe from any of these threats.

The best policy is to consider any product as potentially unsafe. Call your veterinarian or the poison-control number listed in your phone book, particularly if any symptoms of toxicity are exhibited. Victims may paw at their heads or have watering of the eyes, nose, or mouth. Temperature may fluctuate, and difficult breathing or increased thirst can occur. Digestive upsets, with diarrhea, vomiting, or bleeding, can indicate poisoning. Incoordination, convulsions, shock, or coma call for immediate emergency treatment.

Snoopy gags and chokes; does he have something stuck in his throat?

These are common symptoms of tonsillitis, which frequently affects young dogs, especially during teething. Some dogs also display a choking reflex when pulling too hard on leash, causing the collar to irritate the trachea. Of course, something may be stuck in Snoopy's throat, and this possibility should not be overlooked.

If Snoopy is past middle age, these symptoms may also indicate more serious problems, so a checkup is in order.

Why does Daisy eat grass?

Dogs will sometimes eat grass when they have a gastric upset or as a "tonic," similar to their owners' taking castor oil in the spring. Others just seem to graze now and then and, because it doesn't hurt Daisy, you can just let her munch till the cows come home.

Do dogs get cancer?

Dogs not only share good times with us; sometimes they share the bad. They can suffer the same organic maladies that plague us. Our pets can develop diabetes, cataracts, strokes, and heart disease, as well as all forms of cancers and other disorders. Treatments are nearly as comprehensive as in human medicine, with the more advanced forms available at specialized clinics and veterinary teaching hospitals.

Because few owners have health insurance for their dogs, the major stumbling block is cost. If you can afford chemotherapy, dialysis, or a pacemaker for your dog when he needs it, however, the technology is available.

Can Marmaduke catch my cold? Can my baby get worms from him?

With infectious and transmissible conditions, there tends to be little crossing of species lines. So you can pet Marmaduke and allow him to kiss you without fear that either of you will infect the other. Viruses such as parvo or canine distemper can cause disease only in dogs, as human colds or poliovirus affect only people. The rare exception is the rabies virus, which can infect any mammal, a fact that has resulted in great emphasis on prevention by vaccination.

Most bacterial, fungal, and parasitic diseases are also limited: they can't cross to another species and survive. A few exceptions include the omnipresent *Streptococcus* germ that can cause sore throats in pups or kids. One form of ringworm fungus can be passed from dog to human and back again. External parasites such as fleas and ticks prefer dogs, but, if they become hungry enough, they'll feast on human blood instead.

No worms are transmitted from dogs to humans. Under very poor sanitary conditions, humans can pick up worms, not from the dog itself, but from the same culprit that infests the dog, that is, larva passing through an open sore or ingestion of contaminants. With proper cleanliness and veterinary care, Marmaduke won't share his problems with you or your family.

Why does my dog have an irregular heartbeat?

Normal, healthy dogs have a heartbeat that varies from fast to slow. These variations are nothing to be alarmed about. If you notice a consistently speedier heart rate, your vet may want to examine your dog.

My vet said Patches has hip dysplasia. Is he going to die?

Many owners do not even realize their pet is dysplastic until he begins limping and they have him x-rayed. Certain breeds, particularly the large, heavy-boned type, have a higher predisposition for this deformity. *Hip dysplasia* (improper development of the joint) has been shown to exist, in varying degrees, in every breed known in America, except the *racing* Greyhound.

Most dysplastic dogs can live a normal life, with little or no discomfort. Patches should not be bred, however, because the genetic tendency to hip dysplasia would be passed to his puppies. All males and females should be checked for this and other hereditary diseases before breeding.

Mild cases may show a transient lameness at about nine to ten months of age, flashing you a warning signal to have radiographs taken. After that time, no symptoms may occur until middle or old age, when arthritic changes develop. In more serious cases, the dog may become crippled and suffer debilitating pain. Although several surgical procedures can be performed to alleviate pain, dogs with severe hip dysplasia often must be euthanized. New procedures for treating bone disease, including veterinary chiropractic and acupuncture, may extend his pain-free life and should be considered as an alternative to euthanasia.

Dysplasia can also occur in the elbow or shoulder joint. Your vet will discuss ways to ease any pain Patches may exhibit and your pet's long-term prognosis. Most likely you will be able to enjoy Patches's company for many years to come.

Why does my puppy limp every once in a while?

Young ones tend to overdo, thinking their bodies are invincible. Just like your son in Little League, your pup may have pulled a leg muscle or bruised a shoulder sliding into home plate.

Children often have "growing" pains, and some puppies have similar complaints. A disease called *panosteitis* (or, commonly, "pano") can afflict young dogs, particularly during periods of rapid growth in large breeds. Pano causes pain in the long bones and can travel from leg to leg and back again. The good news about this problem is that the disease is temporary and is outgrown by adulthood. Don't assume pano is the cause of lameness, however. Ask your vet to make the diagnosis to make sure it isn't a cracked bone, hip dysplasia, or another serious problem.

Should I give my dog heartworm preventive? How dangerous are heartworms?

Mosquitoes transmit the disease through their bloodthirsty habits, transferring it to a healthy dog from an infected one. Immature heartworms, called *microfilariae,* are carried in the blood vessels. When consumed by the mosquito as it feeds, they change into infective larvae. During the mosquito's subsequent meal, they are injected into the next dog.

After transmittal to the next victim, the larvae grow into adult worms in about two hundred days. They settle in the heart chambers and major pulmonary blood vessels, producing blockage to blood flow and pathological changes in the tissues.

Adult female heartworms grow to as much as ten to fourteen inches, with males about half that length, and both may live five years. The female can produce thousands of microfilariae, evildoers that are transferred to the next host dog, ad infinitum.

First symptoms are often loss of weight with a dull, brittle hair coat. An infected dog may tire easily, showing weakness, a persistent cough, or labored breathing. Victims may vomit blood from ruptured lungs. Chronic infestation will result in congestive heart failure, cirrhosis of the liver, and death.

At one time, heartworm was seen only in dogs in the deep South. Now, there is scarcely an area that is safe. Treatment is available, but it is expensive and not without danger. Because heartworm is simply and effectively prevented by medication, each dog should be tested and then dosed religiously by pill or liquid. This was previously a daily routine; a recent drug innovation allows dogs to be treated on a once-a-month basis. Pets *must* be tested before the preventive is begun, and dosage instructions should be followed implicitly.

Why does Beau have bad breath?

Bad teeth or gums can cause the problem of breath odor when tartar (plaque) creates gingivitis (red, swollen, infected gums). As the

gums are pushed back to expose the dental roots, the teeth die and rot. Your dog's teeth should be cleaned regularly; otherwise, Beau won't attract any Belles.

Chronic tonsillitis can also cause bad breath. For the dog's health, as well as the sake of your offended nose, let his vet check him and prescribe treatment.

I saw a toothpaste for dogs. They've got to be kidding!

Dogs need dental care too and should have their teeth scaled and/or brushed regularly (at least once a week). Dry food and knucklebones help keep the teeth clean, but more effort is needed along the gum lines. Use a soft brush (his own, not yours!) and a paste made from baking soda and water. A doggy toothpaste (also not yours, as it will upset a dog's stomach) can make those pearly teeth sparkle. If necessary, use a scaler to remove any plaque buildup or schedule your pet's dental cleaning by the vet just as you schedule your own at the dentist's.

Do dogs get toothaches, and do they lose their teeth?

Dog teeth are highly resistant to caries (cavities), even if they enjoy a hot fudge sundae now and then. Canine tooth problems mainly involve buildup of plaque, until it nearly covers the tooth. This is accompanied by gingivitis and, finally, exposed tooth roots that die, becoming foul-smelling and causing discomfort. The dog drools and is off his food and prone to chronic tonsillitis, which causes him to gag and vomit.

Continual care to prevent plaque eliminates most of these problems. But once the tooth is dead and infected, it must come out. Your dog will have to have anesthesia during a short hospital stay for extractions, but he'll feel much better when he arrives home. The smaller dogs, especially those with exaggeratedly tiny muzzles (forty-two teeth are crowded into even a three-pound Chihuahua's mouth) are most plagued with tooth loss as they age. But dogs do very little chewing and, even if your pet has many—or in some cases all—of his teeth extracted, he'll do fine with soft food, even without dentures. Some grumpy dogs still manage to "gum" people.

Dental surgery is a new field in veterinary medicine, with root canals and crowns a possibility. In fact, one guard dog had a new gold canine tooth inserted after his own broke. Most people, however, don't have access to a specialist or don't want to spend the money such treatment costs and simply have the affected teeth removed. With good care, your pet's teeth can last his entire life.

Willie looks as if he has double teeth in some spots. Is this possible?

Some puppies retain their milk teeth even after the adult ones begin to erupt at four to seven months. These baby teeth should be pulled: they are dead and serve no purpose except to misalign the adult teeth as they appear. They have small root systems and are easily extracted by your vet.

I've bathed Smokey; why does he still stink?

Check out his ears. If they're infected or full of wax, he may give off a strong, acrid doggy odor. Clean out ears (see Chapter 7) or take Smokey to the vet for treatment. Releasing overfull anal glands also gives off a very rank odor.

Is a cold, wet nose really an indication of good health?

Not necessarily. Although the nose can become dry and warm with a fever, other factors can cause this as well, such as a very hot day. And a dog with a cold, wet nose may be harboring a serious problem. Other symptoms—such as fever, listlessness, or a lack of appetite—are much more reliable.

What should I do if my dog vomits or has diarrhea?

These symptoms can indicate anything from a mild gastric upset to a more serious problem. They can be caused by overeating, change in diet or water, stress, worms, toxic substances, and various viruses. Kaopectate will help control a mild case, along with limiting water and withholding food for a day. As he improves, give the dog small meals of cooked rice, with boiled hamburger, or cottage cheese. If the symptoms do not cease, blood appears in the stool, or temperature elevates, take him to your vet.

Sugar gets nervous at the vet's. What can I do to help calm her?

No one likes facing a situation that sometimes means pain. Perhaps the odors clinging to a medical office (alcohol, blood, disinfectant) stimulate the memory of past discomfort. On your trips to the vet clinic to pick up heartworm pills or flea spray, take Sugar with you and ask the staff to pet her: no poking, prodding, or giving shots, just a nice visit. If you have more than one dog, take the others along for the ride and a lollipop.

Don't feed Sugar before her veterinary appointments. Tingling nerves can tie stomachs in knots, making the situation more uncomfortable and sometimes resulting in nausea and housebreaking accidents. Then Sugar may associate a scolding as well as pain with being at the vet's.

The breeder told me Buddy has only one testicle and suggested neutering him. Will this make him less "macho"?

It is not rare for a male puppy to retain one or both testicles in the abdomen (*cryptorchidism*). Breeders usually detect this before the pup is old enough to be sold and inform buyers, although a testicle that is in normal position can be "pulled up" occasionally after the age of eight weeks.

Neutering Buddy eliminates the possibility of testicular cancer, which sometimes occurs years later in the retained testicle. Cryptorchid dogs should not be bred because the condition is often passed to progeny. Although Buddy won't be able to sire puppies after surgery, he will be just as masculine as any other male if the procedure is done at or after puberty. In fact, only you and your vet (and Buddy) will know for sure.

Why does my dog scratch so much?

If you have eliminated fleas and allergies from the picture, dry skin is a possibility. Add a vitamin E capsule and a spoonful of vegetable oil to your pet's food daily. Dogs that live indoors in the dry winter months and those that are bathed too frequently often develop dry, itchy skin. Do not overbathe, and use only shampoos that are correct for his coat and condition. Nongreasy spray-on moisturizers help.

How much exercise does Baron need?

Enough to keep him fit and content. This varies from breed to breed and from dog to dog, just as it does with their owners. If he's fat and sassy, Baron's probably not receiving enough exercise; if he's lean and mean, maybe you're allowing him to run too much. Keep an eye on his physique and notice his mental attitude. Baron doesn't have to look like the guys at Muscle Beach, but he'll be happier and so will you if he can "flex his biceps" now and then.

How long do most dogs live? What is the record?

Small breeds usually outlive the giants, and the life span seems to decrease as size increases. Although there are claims of dogs living up to thirty-four years, the oldest dog recorded in the *Guinness Book of World Records* was a Queensland Heeler named Bluey, who lived in Australia. The dog herded cattle and sheep for twenty years and finally was euthanized at the age of twenty-nine years, five months.

Many huge dogs—Great Danes, Irish Wolfhounds, or Borzois—

begin to show signs of aging at seven to eight years; the majority of middle-size dogs (such as German Shepherds, Cockers, or Labs) keep active until around ten. Chihuahuas, Toy Poodles, small terriers, and other tinies may still be running circles around you when they're fifteen. Reaching their respective peaks, they begin to slow down, sleeping more and playing less.

Of course, each dog is an individual. Some live far longer than the average and others much less. But no matter what the age, when you lose someone you love, it's too soon.

Why does Mitzi shake her head?

Perhaps there is a fly in her ear. The most likely cause, however, is an ear infection (*otitis*). Besides shaking her head, she may also paw at her ear or rub it against furniture or the floor. Check whether the ear canal is inflamed, has a discharge, or has an offensive odor. Pain can be severe, and Mitzi may cry from the discomfort or carry her head tipped. Her veterinarian can clean the ear and prescribe treatment.

To avoid repeated infections, take care to keep her ears clean and dry. Place a wad of cotton in the canals while she is being bathed and dry them after swimming. Gently clean out any wax accumulation using a cloth or cotton dampened with mineral oil. Chronic otitis can lead to unpleasant complications including hard-to-cure inner-ear infections or conditions such as obliterated ear canals and hematomas, both of which require surgery.

Why do dogs pant?

Dogs perspire only through their noses and footpads. Their major method of body cooling is allowing heat to escape from the moist surfaces of the mouth and tongue. The more area exposed to the air, the better the heat exchange. Harder panting turns up the air-conditioning. Unfortunately, this is not a very efficient system; dogs overheat easily.

In addition, when they're nervous or upset, dogs pant as they "sweat it out."

Checkers is allergic to fleas. What can I do?

Most important, prevent them. Talk to your vet about the most reliable methods of flea control and stick to them faithfully. One flea bite, and Checkers can scratch himself raw in no time. Read the section on fleas in Chapter 7 (p. 76). If allergies become severe, your vet may prescribe medication for your pet. The fleas must be eliminated, however; otherwise the medication will not be effective.

What other things can they be allergic to?

Just like people, dogs can be allergic to foods, pollens, molds, plants, grasses, house dust, insects, materials or chemicals such as dyes or soaps, and many other substances. But whereas people usually have respiratory symptoms (red runny eyes, sneezing), dogs generally exhibit allergies in the skin. They appear as if their skin is on fire, because they lick, rub, chew, and gnaw at themselves constantly, causing discoloration, loss of hair, and eventually open, weeping sores. Symptoms are often seasonal.

Some veterinary clinics can skin-test to identify the allergen and desensitize the dog. Most allergic animals, however, react to many substances. There are medications your vet can prescribe that will give the dog relief from the symptoms until allergy season is over.

Every summer, Muffy gets hot spots. What causes them, and what can I do to make her feel better?

Hot spots is the common name for the sores created by self-mutilation in allergic dogs. Muffy may worry at one spot on her body, chewing or licking, licking, licking. A loss of hair will occur, and what appeared to be a normal, healthy skin one day may erupt into an angry, oozing sore the next.

Topical medications, such as powders or ointments, are licked off. A trip to the vet clinic for allergy shots or pills (usually cortisone or antihistamines) can give temporary relief. Although you can't prevent allergies entirely, you can help minimize symptoms by proper grooming. Dogs with thick, woolly undercoats are more prone to hot spots. Comb out (do not clip) all that dead wool in the spring and summer.

I found a lump on my pet. What does that mean?

A lump or mass, no matter where it appears, should always be checked by your veterinarian. Dogs can develop cysts and boils as well as benign growths such as fatty tumors. Malignancies can also occur, however, that need immediate attention. A stitch in time . . .

My vet says Gretchen has a heart murmur. Will this be dangerous to her? Can I still breed her?

If Gretchen is less than two months old, have her reexamined in a few weeks. Occasionally, puppies have heart murmurs that disappear with time. Even if the murmur remains, it isn't necessarily a crisis. A *murmur* is just an abnormal heart sound that may be heard in dozens of cardiac abnormalities. Some are very mild conditions that allow a dog to live a long and normal life. Others can be caused by severe cardiovascular problems, which sentence the dog to puniness, inactivity, and even death. Veterinary cardiologists can make a specific diagnosis.

Gretchen should be spared the strain of motherhood. Not only could her heart condition worsen, it might also be inherited by her puppies.

What should I do if I see a dog hit by a car?

Approach cautiously, speaking soothingly. Even your own dog may bite you if dazed or in pain, so be prepared to muzzle a large dog or place a thick bath towel or a rug over a small one. Covering the eyes helps calm a frightened dog while allowing you to restrain her physically and avoid being bitten.

Cautiously look for any obvious injuries, but don't prod or manipulate too much. Hemorrhage can be stemmed with direct pressure (a handkerchief or sock). On a leg, apply a tourniquet (panty hose is good for this). Ask another person to call a vet to let him know you're on your way. It's also wise to have someone knock on several doors to see whether the dog's owner is known. Roll the dog onto a coat or blanket or, if the animal is very large, a plank or board before lifting. Severe injuries are not always obvious, so victims should always be examined by a veterinarian.

Emergency treatment of trauma is not free, and, if the owner is not found, you will be responsible for payment. But no dog should be left to suffer, and any compassionate vet would be willing at least to start treatment before the owner is found. If necessary, a critically wounded stray may have to be euthanized, a procedure often performed by vets for a minimum fee. Sometimes owners don't appreciate your Good Samaritan efforts, but true animal lovers feel compensated for their trouble, even when *they* must pay.

What are the symptoms of shock?

Check the gums or the inside of the lower eyelid; normally, these tissues are a healthy pink. In shock, they become very pale or even grayish white. As shock progresses, the dog will exhibit shallow, rapid breathing with disorientation and/or semiconsciousness. Whether caused by pain, toxicity, hemorrhage, or internal injuries, shock can kill. Your dog must be treated immediately. Wrap him in a blanket to maintain body heat and rush him to the vet.

What is torsion, and how will I know if it happens?

There is no mistaking gastric torsion when it occurs. When the stomach (which hangs like a hammock) flips over on its long axis, the entrance and exit are shut off. Gas due to bacterial action begins to build. The dog is unable to vomit or defecate to relieve the pressure. As the gas expands, the abdominal area swells to amazing size, often causing the dog to look as if it swallowed a medicine ball. Torsion causes severe pain, and the dog moans and attempts to vomit without success. The twisting also shuts off all of the veins and arteries to the stomach and spleen. This triggers septic shock, which may be irreversible within an hour or two.

Do not wait! Torsion is a killer! Even if it's the middle of the night, call your emergency vet, then leave immediately. The dog must be treated as soon as possible for shock; this treatment is followed by surgery performed to correct the blockage. Often the surgeon will tack the stomach to the abdominal wall so torsion will not recur.

What are true medical emergencies?

Emergencies are conditions that immediately put your dog's life in jeopardy. They are never anticipated, and this is why it is so important to know where you can call for advice and for help day, night, or holiday.

Emergency situations are shock, electric shock, torsion, heat stroke, massive wounds or compound fractures, *anoxia* (lack of air, choking), *dystocia* (severe labor and delivery problems), *hemorrhage* (uncontrollable pumping of blood), and *neurological symptoms* (convulsions, unconsciousness, or paralysis caused by trauma, poisoning, or other pathology). These are *don't wait* situations, whether in the middle of the night or on Christmas Day. It's better to find out at 2:00 A.M. that it isn't an emergency than to find your pet dead in the morning. A caring vet will agree.

10

Schooldays and Recess Time

How soon can I start teaching Rosie good manners? What about obedience or show training?

Teaching good manners starts the minute you bring Rosie home. She can begin to learn *not* to beg, bite, or puddle. Even an eight-week-old puppy can be taught gently and patiently with *lots* of praise to "Sit" and to "Stay" for short periods of time.

The "Sit" and "Stay" commands can be used to stop bad habits before they start, including many of the complaints about pet misbehavior in this chapter. Your veterinarian, for one, will thank you. It's much easier to insert a thermometer or check the throat of a pup that knows "Stay" than one who is a canine yo-yo.

You and Rosie both need time to enjoy her babyhood, however, before becoming serious about training. Puppy kindergarten classes are wonderful socializing experiences for canine toddlers (about two to six months)—and their owners—and also teach the basics of good behavior. It's a toss-up whether pups or people have more fun!

Most owners who are interested in conformation (breed ring) enroll their pup in a class as early as possible (two to three months). *Conformation* (that is, judging the dog on appearance and gait) training can serve as an alternative to puppy classes. Dogs are taught how to stand still, as still as a young one can between kisses and tail wagging by her and oooohs and cuddling by the human participants. She'll learn how to walk on leash and how to behave around other dogs and people and receive a lot of praise doing it!

Most obedience trainers suggest waiting until your dog is five or six months old to begin formal classes. By then, her attention span will have increased enough so that she will be able to learn the exercises without stress.

No matter what your choice in classes, wait until your puppy is fully immunized to enroll, and then train with TLC. Your dog is an adult for ten or more years and a puppy only for a few short months. Enjoy her!

I'm not interested in showing Bullet. Will class training still help him?

One of the most valuable lessons is for you as the trainer: you will gain control of your dog, learn how to remain the dominant party of the relationship, and enjoy your pet more fully. This is why it is important for one of the family to serve as the dog trainer rather than hiring someone else. Bullet should learn to mind *you*, not someone he will never see again, and you should learn how to effect good behavior. Classes provide practice in behaving under any circumstances. Although many dogs mind at home, just like an ornery kid, they sometimes disgrace and embarrass their family in public.

Basic lessons taught in an eight- to ten-week course include the "Sit," "Stand," "Down," "Come," and "Stay" commands. You will also learn how to make Bullet "Heel" so that he won't drag you or twist the leash around your feet. Several of the lessons ("Stay," "Down," "Come") your dog learns in class could save his life and certainly are important for your sanity and that of your friends and neighbors. You can prevent Bullet from becoming an antisocial dropout by teaching him the ABCs at dog school.

Can't Mandy get sick from being around other dogs?

Reputable schools and clubs require registrants to be fully immunized and in good health. The benefits received from classes far outweigh the remote possibility of contagion. If Mandy becomes ill during the course or comes in season and you have to miss more than one class, call the instructor to ask whether you can continue the lessons in the next scheduled session.

Where do I find a dog club? Do I have to become a member?

Training clubs and schools are often listed in the yellow pages or by the Chamber of Commerce. For further sources, ask a veterinarian or write to AKC for suggestions. Clubs usually allow nonmembers to pay a fee and take a course in either obedience or conformation.

There are many reasons to join, however, because being a member makes you part of a group of people who have a common love for dogs. These owners have varied interests in the canine world, with diverse knowledge. Every single thing that affects you and your dog has happened to someone else before. If other members haven't experienced this particular phenomenon, they probably can tell you where to obtain help or information. Dog clubs offer members many other advantages: newsletters, social functions, car pooling to events, and referrals for puppy sales and stud services.

Clubs often host seminars, which give tips on breeding, handling, genetics, tracking, obedience, movement, structure, grooming, behavioral problems, field training, puppy aptitude testing, and countless other subjects.

Among their many activities, one of the main functions of a club is to host shows and trials, giving you an opportunity to learn the world of dog shows firsthand. But, remember, all these events operate under volunteer power, and being a club member is a two-way partnership.

But what's more, a good club is a group of people who cheer each other's successes, give help when one stumbles, or offer a shoulder during a difficult moment. Such an organization provides new and good friends.

How do I get Tasha to come to me when I call?

The obedience instructor can teach you the intricacies of teaching the lesson termed the *recall*. But a good point to remember is to make Tasha *want* to obey. Command the dog to "Sit; Stay." Walk off and call the dog's name, saying "Tasha, 'Come!' " in a happy, enticing tone. Convince Tasha you want her with you more than anything in the world. Give a short jerk on the leash at the same time as you call her. When Tasha reaches you, let her know that she's wonderful, terrific, and sooooo smart!

Don't give a command you can't enforce such as yelling "Come" to an untrained dog who is off leash. All this teaches her is that she doesn't have to obey, and nothing can stop her from running in the other direction. If you are trying to catch Tasha when she accidentally sneaks out the door, don't run after her. This leads to a merry (for her) game of chase, with you as the loser. Instead, run in the opposite direction, calling her name. This diversionary tactic will encourage her to chase *you* instead of the other way around.

Never, *never* correct her when she returns, whether she jumps up plastering you with mud or whether she's been gone for an hour giving you heart failure. Make her always want to respond to your call.

There are no classes or clubs in my area. I'd like Bryn to have some doggie friends; any suggestions?

Start one of your own! AKC can give you tips on starting a dog club if you wish to go the formal route. Otherwise, informal get-to-gethers allowing dogs to play are good opportunities for owners to socialize and swap information. Put an ad in the paper and gather a bunch of sticks, toys, balls, and Frisbees.

Set up a few ground rules: dogs must have shots; owners must be responsible for their own pets; clean up immediately; and so on. Plan activities, whether obedience, conformation, or sports, followed by free play time. Once you start the ball rolling, you'll have plenty of helpers to pick it up and run with it.

He's a good dog, but I can't stop him from jumping up on people. What can I do besides lose my friends?

Dogs prefer to be eye-to-eye with humans. Some people don't mind this, but others object to being hit in the chest by a 150-pound animal or having nylons snagged and clothes covered with muddy paw prints. Several methods of correction can eliminate this bad habit.

Probably the best answer is never to allow a puppy to start. Puppies are so cute that we tend to encourage them to climb on our laps and to jump up. Instead, tell a young one to "Sit" and then bend down to his level, telling him what a marvel he is.

If your dog continues his Baryshnikov leaps, look for a theatrical agent or try saying "Sit!" firmly. When he coils his legs ready for a spring, step quickly back or to the side so he falls on his face, or forward so he flips backward. Loudly say "No! Off!" at the same time. Or catch his front feet when he jumps up, holding him up until he becomes uncomfortable and restless, to reinforce your authority. You can also try turning a bad habit into a lesson, teaching him only to leap when you say "Up!"

I'd like to teach Rory some tricks. Which are the easiest for him to learn?

Dogs love attention, and, if you combine play or tricks with praise, they'll do anything within their physical capabilities to please you. Just observe circus dogs and their talents. Find a book on teaching dogs tricks, or make up your own as you go.

Many dogs, particularly the Sporting breeds, enjoy a rousing game of fetch. Once they catch on, they'll bring anything you want: slippers, newspaper, or a can of beer during the ball game.

Teaching to "Speak" on command is usually simple, because most dogs love to bark. From there, you can progress to telling his age or yours (if he can bark that long without hyperventilating). Other favorites are "Beg" (and here you just taught Rory not to do that!), "Shake," "Dance," "Sing," "Roll over," "Say your prayers," or "Jump through a hoop."

For laughs, you can also switch commands or use hand signals to clue your dog. With this trick, you can entertain kids—and adults— by teaching Rory to lie down when you say "Sit" or yawn when you say "Come."

What kind of collar should I use? Will I have to use one of those awful spike collars in class?

In training classes a slip collar, either nylon or chain, is most often used. This collar communicates in the most humane way as it releases immediately after the correction. The slip collar is only for training and everyday walks and must *never* be left on the dog in your absence because he can catch it on something and choke to death. Use a flat buckle-type for everyday use and to attach tags. Some trainers are also recommending one of the new types of head halters, such as the K-9 Kumalong, Gentle Leader, or Halti.

Occasionally, when the dog outweighs the person training it, the handler needs an advantage such as a pronged or "pinch" collar. This is particularly true when the animal is aggressive or a recalcitrant con artist. The prongs are smoothly rounded (not "spiked") and designed to pinch quickly and release as soon as the dog behaves properly.

But Kaiser is seven years old. Isn't it too late for him to learn anything?

You *can* teach an old dog new tricks! Many dogs aren't enrolled in formal training until middle age or older. Of course, the ones that succeed are those that recognize their master's authority already. If you've allowed Kaiser to run amok, it *can* be too late by seven months.

Each dog is an individual, and some are no longer physically capable of performing the way they would have at a younger age. Within the annals of the American Kennel Club exists the record of a ten-year-old Dalmatian who earned her CD, CDX, and UD within one year of starting her training!

Why does Waldo continue to do things he knows are wrong? I've spanked him and yelled at him, but he keeps on being bad.

Most people correct dogs too late and too long by climbing on the proverbial soapbox. An animal understands only selected words, as evidenced by the capitalized ones in the following discourse:

"WALDO, you are a BAD dog! Why can't you ever do anything I tell you? Why can't you be GOOD instead of BAD? Those were my GOOD shoes. You've got plenty of TOYS. Why can't you PLAY with them and be a GOOD boy?"

By this point Waldo has no idea whether he's GOOD or BAD, and you're pointing to the shoes and saying "TOYS" and "PLAY." Because you're yelling and smacking him at the same time, he's thoroughly confused. Next time you leave the house and tell him to PLAY with his TOYS, you'd better hide your shoes.

Corrections should be made immediately after the fact or on finding evidence of misbehavior. Go to him (don't call him, remember) and take him to the scene of his crime. Use direct eye contact and tell him "No, no, no, *baaaaaad* dog!" in a loud voice. Your displeasure is the worst punishment for your pet. Dogs do not really understand what is "right" or "wrong," and they certainly aren't bad on purpose; they simply have no concept of logic and cannot plot revenge.

If you need to reinforce your authority with a more serious step, grasp the nape of his neck or the mane area if he has long enough hair. Depending on his size and the severity of his trespass, give him a firm shake along with your verbal scolding.

If I shouldn't hit him, what can I do to stop him from chewing?

To "nip" chewing, besides trying the previous method, coat the object of his sweet tooth with Tabasco sauce, Bitter Apple, or asafetida (which produces nausea when licked). Determine when your pet is committing his crimes and stop him before he starts. If it's during teething periods, give him a chew toy or large knucklebone. Crate him when you're away from home, and use this method of correction if chewing occurs when you turn your back for a moment.

How do I keep Pierre off the furniture?

If you don't wish your dog to lie on your furniture, don't let him start. He won't understand that it's all right when you're home alone, but all wrong when you have guests. Place set mousetraps on the sofa and cover them with newspapers. When Pierre leaps on the couch, the traps will spring, making a racket, accentuated by the papers.

If you want to share your comfort with Pierre, but don't want dog hair on all the furniture, "give" him one chair or an end of the couch. Place a blanket on it if you wish and remove it when guests arrive. Be prepared, however, for Pierre to give the evil eye to anyone he discovers on "his" chair.

How can I stop Benji from chasing cars?

Terriers, Hounds, and Sporting and Herding dogs all love the spirit of the chase, although even a Kuvasz may find this "sport" exciting. This annoying and dangerous prank not only is life-threatening to the dog but startles drivers. Many car chasers spring after anything that moves quickly and also frighten joggers and children on bikes.

Attach Benji to a longe lead such as that used in training horses. Work in the yard and wait for his first temptation. As he takes off, brace yourself and flip him on his back, yelling "Noooo!" at the same time. If you can convince a friend to cooperate with you, ask her to drive by slowly. As the culprit hits high gear, she can pelt him with one of several items: a water-filled balloon, a plastic squeeze lemon filled with juice, or a squirt bottle containing a very weak mixture of ammonia and water. These won't hurt him but will dampen his zeal. Another method is to insert pebbles into an aluminum can, seal it with strong tape, and throw it in front of the dog. At the same time, all voices together should chorus a loud "Nooooooo!"

I've been thinking about attack training my dog to guard my family. What do you think about that?

Not much. An attack dog does not belong in a family situation in which he is a "loaded pistol" ready for action. Dogs should only be trained for attack work in controlled environments by knowledgeable handlers. These animals are carefully selected for even temperaments so that they respond immediately to command. Off duty, they are rarely family dogs or children's playmates. Think of the potential danger when Rolf watches "his" boy fighting with a neighbor child, pushing, shoving, and crying.

Most dogs who love their owners instinctively protect them from a real threat, without specialized training, and that's all that's really wanted by the average family. No one wants a dog who's likely to injure a guest, a child, or an innocent stranger. Attack dogs should be left to the experts, such as police officers or security guards.

I don't want our whole relationship to be just walks, training, and discipline. I'd like some more suggestions for playing with Lolly.

Lucky Lolly! Try some of the previously mentioned tricks. Play keep-away or hide her favorite treat. Try hide and seek—put the dog on a "Sit" or "Stay" or ask someone to hold her while you hide and call her. This has the added bonus of being excellent training for tracking. Share everyday activities with Lolly, allowing her to accompany you in the car as long as it's not too hot. Hold conversations with her, first in your language. Then lower yourself to the floor and talk in doggy tones and body language. Offer her your "paw," and wag your "tail." Roll on your back and pant. Note her reactions. At first it may be puzzlement, but, as time goes on, she'll join you in delight, or in an embarrassed attempt to cover up your obviously demented state.

Use your imagination for more ideas. Check the Suggested Reading (pp. 191–92) for a book on this subject.

What can I do to keep my dog healthy and happy?

If he seems as tense as a turkey the day before Thanksgiving, he probably needs to release some of that excess spirit in a romp or a game of ball. Depending on the breed and the individual inclination, a leisurely stroll around the block may suffice, or a half-hour session at a full gallop may be necessary.

In some cities, professional dog walkers assist the busy owner and offer an alternative to midnight outings with frustrated pets.

I'm athletic. Can Hunk join me?

He can't play racquetball, but he can jog, swim, backpack, run beside your bike, and play catch or Frisbee. When you're practicing your golf swing at home or hitting tennis balls against a garage wall, let Hunk retrieve the balls for you. His keen nose can find a golf ball hidden in the rough a lot quicker than you can. It'll give him exercise and relieve you from a tedious chore.

Which toys are safe? Which will keep my dog entertained when I'm not at home?

Put in a store of solid hard rubber balls, large enough so they can't be swallowed or lodged in her throat. Don't give your pet a squeaky toy unless you are certain she can't chew it up and swallow the noisemaker. Chew toys such as the Cressite bones and tugs, resilient nylon and polyurethane toys, or large, raw knucklebones from the butcher can keep a dog content for hours.

What are some really different activities I can share with Sundae?

How about sledding? If Sundae is a Samoyed or other Nordic-type dog, she'll relish being harnessed to a sled filled with kids, and many other breeds enjoy this as well. Pulling weights or wagons is an alternative. Hiking and mountain climbing with dogs are allowed in certain parks. Be sure to check rules before driving four hundred miles to the area, however.

Some clubs have obstacle or agility courses, teams for scent hurdle or fly-ball racing, precision drill teams, or fun matches.

Are dogs really natural swimmers?

Many are, although a few dogs hate the water. Most of the Sporting breeds are natural water retrievers, and others, such as Newfoundlands, have the sea in their blood too. Although they don't attempt the sidestroke or butterfly, they are the original dog paddlers and great at the running dive.

Most people who have a home pool don't allow their dog to swim in it because the hair clogs the filter and nails can rip the liner. Whether or not you encourage water sports, teach him to get out of the pool and make certain that your pet cannot possibly infiltrate the area when you aren't there. Each year pets (as well as children) drown because they jump into the pool and exhaust themselves trying to climb the slippery side. Another danger exists if they walk on the cover because it can collapse, pulling the dog along and entangling it under water.

I've found that my kids toss the toy aside and play with the box. What kind of homemade toys can I come up with for my dogs?

If you allow your pets to play with old shoes, boil a leather one to make it harder and more durable. Knot socks or old belts (with buckles removed) for tug toys. Socks are particularly interesting if they have a ball knotted inside them, and these don't roll immediately under the couch or down the stairs. Plastic milk jugs and soft drink liter bottles are wonderful for flipping into the air, particularly if they're filled with edible noisemakers such as dog treats. Whether they are purchased or homemade, check toys regularly and throw away those that have loose pieces or sharp edges.

Build some wooden platforms of various heights in the backyard by placing waterproof boards on sturdy legs, such as railroad ties. Your dogs will love playing "king of the mountain."

I have a Greyhound, and I'd like to learn about racing and lure coursing.

Professional racing dogs are raised by breeders for that specific purpose. Many sight hound owners, however, do race and course for their own and their dogs' enjoyment. These dogs are pure racing machines, possessing sleek bodies, and are a solid muscle mass.

The dogs tear after a lure made out of white plastic that is drawn by means of a pulley on a course of five hundred to twelve hundred yards. They are judged on speed, agility, enthusiasm, following ability, and endurance. You should attempt to find a group interested in this activity, but, even before you join their pursuit, you can begin training by encouraging these characteristics in your Greyhound.

I hunt and I'd like to have Odie join me. Any special tips?

If Odie is a Sporting dog or Hound, his instincts should make him a natural, and all you'll have to do is encourage them. If Odie is a Bernese Mountain Dog, you may have more fun—and success—playing checkers with him.

Hunting is a pursuit for specialists. Bird hunters need a busy, active dog with a great nose to search ahead. Bird dogs either point or flush the game, as well as find and retrieve it after the shot. The rabbit hunter's companion should be persistent in following a ground scent and voicing his find. Hunting raccoon (which is done at night) requires good hounds that bay loudly so you know where they are on the trail and when they have treed their quarry. Conversely, duck hunters want their dogs to keep still and quiet until a duck is shot, when they retrieve from water of any temperature. Hunting deer with a dog is illegal, so keep Odie home during that season, particularly if he likes to run deer or looks like a deer.

Each type of hunting dog has been selectively bred for these specialized traits over many generations. They "do their thing" instinctively, with only a bit of practice and encouragement, along with minimal training for fine-tuning.

Even the best coon hunting dog, to say nothing of your Bernese, would disappoint you in a duck blind. But if your dog is athletic and obedient and your idea of hunting is just to go out in the fresh air for a long walk, there is no reason Odie can't accompany you.

11

What Makes Him Tick?

Ginger's afraid of other dogs. Why? What can I do about this?

Although this phenomenon can be caused by a bad experience, usually it's the effect of removing a puppy from its littermates too early. Experts have shown that young dogs need sibling companionship until they are eight to ten weeks old. Pups need the adventures of chewing on each other's ears, falling over each other into the food bowl, and playing puppy tag. Breeders with an "only pup" and new owners with pets younger than eight weeks must provide the canine social life.

As soon as your pup is immunized, introduce her to other dogs. Walk her in the park, or enter her in a puppy kindergarten class.

There is hope even for wallflowers like Ginger. She must learn she is a dog, not just a four-legged extension of your human family. First, let her watch other dogs having fun from a "safe" distance. As she begins to relax, plan canine get-togethers. Arrange a "blind date" for her by choosing a calm, nonthreatening "gentledog" to accompany her on a stroll. Buy her a new toy that requires more than one to play.

Throw parties. Relax—let her discover the joys of chasing or fighting over custody of a stick. Let her enjoy being a dog.

After all, there are special benefits to a dog's life: she can bask in the sun, snore when there's company, and be content with minimal possessions. Ginger has no job she hates, no unemployment lines, no sweating over a hot stove, no punk rock kids, no worries to keep her awake.

My dog won't let anyone except me touch him. Why is Fritz so shy?

Canine shrinking violets often owe their touch-me-not behavior to a shy parent or ancestor. Dogs can become "kennel-shy," however, when they are left on the shelf too long, unless exposed to new experiences and given individual attention. Some enfold themselves in a protective cocoon after suffering a trauma, particularly at puberty. Whatever the reason, as shy people can tell you, it's no fun sitting on the sidelines watching the rest of the world dance by.

Try to build his confidence; gentle obedience training usually helps boost a sagging ego. Give Fritz an easy chore and praise him when he does well. Visit shopping centers and allow him to adjust to people bustling around. As he calms, ask some of the shoppers to pet him. Although Fritz may never become a social butterfly, he may learn there is nothing to fear from the approach of a stranger.

Are all show dogs high-strung?

Of course not—just like human performers and athletes, some are as laid-back as Johnny Carson, and others are temperamental and snooty.

They're individuals, just as we are, and it depends on how they're raised and handled.

Put your dog on a pedestal and don't allow him to play, crate him twenty-four hours a day, or treat him like a pampered toy, and you can turn any dog into a psychotic one, show dog or not. Most show dogs, in fact, are outgoing because of the exposure they receive; they're often calm, well-behaved companions because they have an outlet for their energy and a purpose to their lives. And most love to be "on stage."

When will Dickens stop being a puppy?

We humans tend to wish away time, then regret it as soon as we're granted our wish. Dogs under a year are very much like human toddlers. They're curious and exuberant and have at least ten times as much energy as we do.

If you are wondering when he will sleep through the night and understand the word *no*, the answer is, not soon enough. If it's when he will stop chasing squirrels and walk calmly on leash, sooner than you think. If it's growing out of his puppy cuteness, too soon. But if it's the end of greeting you with unbridled joy and a constant eagerness to accompany you everywhere, ideally, never.

My pup nips me. Is that a sign he'll grow up to be mean?

Many pups prefer to do their teething on human hands and ankles, sinking their needle-sharp "milk" teeth into unsuspecting portions of our anatomy. They also are playing, as they would with their littermates. It should, of course, be stopped (it hurts!) but isn't necessarily a sign of a future as a junkyard dawg.

The nipping should be corrected by a sharp "No!" and by substitution of an acceptable toy. If he persists, stronger measures can accompany the verbal displeasure. Shake him by the ruff of his neck or hold his muzzle closed, tightly enough to be uncomfortable. These are dominant actions exhibited by canine mothers. They work, they're simple, and they're painless.

Some herding dogs herd people—in place of cattle or sheep—by nipping at their heels. Teach children to hold still and say "No," rather than running, which signals these dogs to begin their "job."

Tuffy bites at me when I try to correct him. What should I do?

Don't let a bad habit start. If your pup is actually biting aggressively, "nip" the hostility in the bud. Enroll him in puppy reform school. Do not allow him to gain dominance.

It's a lot harder to curtail the biting of an eighty-pound one-year-old than a twenty-pound three-month baby. At this early stage you can sit on him if necessary to maintain the upper position! Once dogs learn to submit to your will, they maintain that attitude even when they outweigh you.

Why do dogs sniff embarrassing places on themselves and on people?

A dog's keenest sense is that of smell; its nose is a canine radar detector. Things we don't even whiff are multiplied a thousandfold to them. Little wonder their method of identification is sniffing rather than a handshake and an introduction. Dogs are stupendous at detecting characteristics, including fear, with their noses. Unfortunately, certain areas such as the armpit, foot, or groin emit an irresistible invitation to their sniffers.

To curb this action, say "No" and command the dog to "Sit." Offer your "paw" for a thorough smell feast.

Ulysses insists on rolling in smelly things. Why is he so disgusting?

Sometimes it seems the smellier it is, the better dogs like it. This may be a throwback to the wild, when canines covered their own individual scent with the stronger smell of something else. Thus, garbage and dead animals may draw Ulysses like the voice of the Sirens.

Walk him by such a magnetic force and yell "No!" at the first twitch of a nostril. Turn in the other direction, yanking hard on the leash, and flip him over if necessary. If he persists in being a "stinker," keep Ulysses on leash and under control.

Why is Hilda so afraid of thunderstorms and firecrackers?
How can I help her get over this fear?

Many dogs just seem to be born sensitive to loud noises, perhaps because they have an overdeveloped startle reflex. Because our world is full of booms and bangs, a supersensitive dog can potentially spend her life under the bed. Several methods may be attempted. Do not coddle Hilda, seeming to approve of her actions. Ignore the noise and continue with normal activities, talking calmly.

Because this "gun-shy" condition is disastrous to Sporting dogs, hunters occasionally acclimate their charges to noise, starting at puppyhood, by firing a blank pistol in the air at feeding time. Such a situation can be simulated by banging two pots or by playing at low volume a recording of a thunderstorm.

Some dogs have such a deep-seated fear of loud noises, however, that it is difficult to eradicate. It is painful to cause terror to someone you love, and most owners elect to live with the dog's fear and to control it rather than to attempt a cure. During storms (and on July 4), place Hilda in her crate with a toy. Sometimes it helps to cover the crate, calming her and further muting the noise. Tranquilizers, prescribed by Hilda's veterinarian, can also help.

How can I make Gunner friendlier to people, and not so aggressive?

Socializing from puppyhood, in the same manner as for the shy dog, is the best preventive of aggression. Many times, owners unknowingly encourage canine hostility. It is so cute to see a small pup popping off like a capgun as people approach. This is when it must be halted, however, before the toy pistol becomes a cannon ready to explode and destroy.

Enroll Gunner in an obedience course and teach him to obey you without pause. He must learn to tolerate the approach of others. The professional trainer has met many aggressive dogs, and he can give you sound advice in defusing your weapon.

Be careful that you aren't unknowingly encouraging the behavior. Owners often stroke and pet a dog who is growling or barking, thinking they are soothing the aggression. The dog interprets this as praise for his behavior. He should be told "No!" and lifted up by the collar, immediately stopping his surliness.

Are some breeds naturally mean? I've heard that some will "turn" on you.

An aggressive dog is one that has not been properly disciplined as a pup and is used to having things his own way. A few years later, when someone tries to force him to do something, his dominance over people is demonstrated by his snapping jaws. This startles and terrorizes the owners, and a vicious circle starts. The more you let him control the situation, the more he will enforce it. This is why it is vital for the owner to gain the upper hand when the dog is just a pup.

According to statistics, it is more likely a human member of your family will turn on you than your dog. All normal dogs, whether shy or aggressive to outsiders, are friendly to members of their own household. Nevertheless, insanity can affect more than humans; canines can suffer mental disturbances too. Instinctive protection against abuse can also cause a dog to attack its owners.

No blanket judgment can be made for any breed. Dogs are individuals, just as people are, as discussed in Chapter 2.

Is it true that a barking dog never bites?

Not while it's barking! As soon as the noise stops, watch out.

Learn to watch for various canine signals. A growl or snarl is often more threatening than a bark, because barks can be invitations to play or vocalized excitement, although these warnings should be taken seriously. Other danger signs of aggression are hackles (hair above the withers) raised, lifted lip, direct eye contact, ears and tail carried high. The hackles, ears, and tail make the dog appear bigger, and an aggressive animal actually appears to rise up on its toes.

I'm a dog lover, but I don't trust my neighbor's dog. He slinks around looking as if he'd like to jump me when my back's turned. What's the matter with him?

Fear biters, dogs who bite from terror, are the most dangerous type and can never be trusted. Their posture is lower-stanced than the aggressive dog's—the head may be carried down, with ears laid back against the skull. Movement is like that of a panther and just as menacing. Although aggressive dogs usually can be brought under control, the fear biter is often incurable.

Certainly, not all fearful dogs are vicious; many resort to submissive tactics such as running away or cringing. But, if cornered, they may be pushed to "protect" themselves with their teeth. Ignore the dog, and tell children to stay away from him. Ask your neighbor to keep his dog under restraint, but, because many owners do not realize the potential danger, it may be up to *you* to erect the fence.

What should I tell my child to do if she's ever attacked by a dog?

Few things are more frightening to a child—or an adult—than a threat from a vicious dog. Although the first instinct is to run, scream, and flail her arms, the best thing to do is to stand still. Dogs instinctively chase moving objects. She should avoid eye contact (a challenge of dominance) but face the dog and watch him out of the corner of her eye. Finally, she can begin to back up slowly. Tell her to talk calmly, trying to soothe the animal's ruffled "feathers."

These measures also work with grown-ups. Adults, however, can also attempt another ploy used by many joggers if pressed. Rather than holding still, stand tall and move toward him. Stamp your feet, look him aggressively in the eye, and yell "No!" in a growling tone. You may just surprise him into turning tail and running from the new "boss dog."

There is a difference between a threat and an actual attack, however. Victims should protect the most vulnerable parts of their bodies. Fold your arms, prepared to lift them over your face should the dog lunge forward. Try to curl up in a corner with only your back exposed to afford you the most protection.

How can I shut Spike up? He barks at leaves, squirrels, everybody, and everything.

Some dogs bark just to keep themselves company. This is a common problem with dogs that are bored from being tied outside or being left alone all day.

Others bark to evoke your appearance, and, when you come to the door to quiet them, they bark out of excitement. When you leave, they bark again to bring you back. This annoying habit is a major cause of trouble with neighbors.

To sour Spike's taste for barking, keep a squeeze container of lemon juice nearby. Every time he opens his mouth, blast him with a generous gulp of lemons. If he is sensitive to sharp noises, use the can of pebbles described on pages 109–10.

Provide Spike with toys, or his only entertainment may be right under his nose. Don't doom him to a boring existence—let him perform a chore or take him for a run. Use the secret mothers of toddlers have known for centuries: wear him out, so he has no energy left for mischief.

As a last resort, electronic antibark collars or debarking surgery is a better solution than driving your neighbor to call the police or—worse—shoot or poison your dog.

Dirty Harry digs holes in my yard. How can I stop him?

Some dogs, especially terriers, are driven to dig, and they aren't particular whether they're tunneling after a fierce badger in the woods or burrowing for an imaginary mouse in your prize-winning petunia patch. If you determine the cause of his excavations to be instinct rather than boredom, confine him to an unlandscaped area where he can mine until there's no ground left. That'll make his day! Or you can try cementing the yard and painting it green.

Maverick steals food off my countertop. What can I do?

Never leave temptation within reach. You wouldn't leave a cookie at eye level with a toddler and expect it to remain long. A dog's willpower lasts about as long as a two-year-old's. (It doesn't.) Although some dogs can be trained to behave impeccably even if they're starving while the juicy steak is sending out a tantalizing aroma, most give in swiftly. Why not? Maverick doesn't know that he has ruined your barbecue or that the cake he's gobbled is for your boss's birthday.

You can scold, you can yell, you can smack Maverick, and you'll still eat peanut butter instead of steak. Wouldn't it be easier to place the temptation in the oven or on top of the refrigerator? Then all you have to worry about is the cat.

Do dogs really hate cats?

Quite the contrary! They often love them, and they particularly love to chase them. Dogs, and cats too, have an instinct to chase that which runs from them. It's a timeless game that passes from generation

to generation. If dogs are raised with cats, most become quite accepting of each other and sometimes good friends.

Some dogs are instinctive cat killers, however, so know your dog before subjecting a kitten to a possible death sentence.

Lambie is soooooo sweet, but she wants to be petted twenty-four hours a day. I feel mean pushing her away because she looks so mournful. Any suggestions?

Lambie nudges, and you obey. Who's dishing out the orders? Dogs are good con artists, and this is a clever method of subtly dominating you, without your even realizing it. Giving and receiving affection are among the major joys of having a pet, but caresses should be doled out at your wish, not your dog's command. Before you yield to her wishes, ask her to do something for you. Tell her "Shake," "Sit," or "Bring me the paper"; then follow up with a "Good Lambie" and a couple of pats. If she persists, put her on a "Down; Stay." See the advantages of being the boss?

Schedule a time especially for her. Throw a ball, teach her tricks, or engage in a wrestling match. If she receives plenty of attention during "her time," you won't feel guilty when you don't allow her to nudge you every two words while you're reading a book.

I think Lassie can tell time. Is that possible?

Dogs seem to have a sixth sense of when something should occur. It used to be a common sight for dogs to be lined up along the various schoolbus stops. Modern dogs wait at the door or window for their pals to come home. They nudge you at precisely 10:25 P.M. for their bedtime treat. They know before you do when you're going to hang up the phone and pay attention to them or when it's time to pick up Dad at the station.

Not only do dogs have an inborn sense of routine, but they observe our subtle signals. If you put on lipstick only when you go out of the house, Lassie will become overjoyed when you reach for the tube. She knows it means a ride in the car. As you lay out the place mat for your preschooler's lunch, she realizes he'll soon be bursting in the door, ready for a romp. And, after her nighttime walk, you watch the news, have a snack, and go to bed. Watch yourself for tipoffs, but don't take all the mystique away from Lassie. Bill her as Nostradamus, the canine psychic.

PART THREE

LIVING WITH YOUR DOG

12
The Travel Bug

I'm going on vacation soon. What can I do with Gretel?

Several choices are open to dog owners who have itchy feet and want to travel. Much as we love our animals, they do have daily demands that must be met. Therefore, because part of having a vacation is basking in freedom from responsibility, most people board their pets. Many others believe the joy they receive from having Hansel or Gretel with them on vacation outweighs the few duties involved and gives both owners and dogs an excuse to get out in the fresh air.

If neither of these choices is feasible, consider hiring a dog sitter or asking a friend or relative to watch Gretel. Another possibility is to take her with you to your destination and find a boarding kennel there. This may be the best of all choices. You can visit Gretel and take her with you on a relaxing hike in the woods or for a visit to Aunt Dor, who also loves dogs. But the day you visit Disney World, you can enjoy yourself from sunup to sundown without worrying about what Gretel's doing to your motel room.

I travel extensively on my job. How do I choose a good boarding kennel for Houdini?

Dogs are often boarded at times other than vacations. These include disruptive periods such as holidays, family moves, or home remodeling; while the owners are entertaining, on business trips, or on weekend getaways; and during a bitch's heat cycle. This means you must select a kennel you can count on.

Although veterinary clinics occasionally offer boarding facilities, their space is often small and confining because extensive exercise is not sanctioned for recuperating patients. The vets and their staff have busy schedules and usually do not encourage visitors. For elderly or chronically ill pets, however, the proximity of medical services is a big plus.

You can ask your vet or other dog owners for recommendations. Look in the yellow pages for professional boarding kennels, and make appointments to see several of them. When you visit, look for a kennel manager who has a natural rapport and love for dogs, not one who begrudges every moment spent with them.

Most kennels are extremely noisy—one bark sets off a domino reaction. Although kennel workers do not have time to pick up droppings the moment they land, runs should be cleaned several times a day and disinfected between clients. A vet should be on call. Check to make sure pets are protected from neighboring boarders. Fencing should be strong, secure, and high enough to keep in an Olympic high jumper. If Houdini is an escape artist, ask about a topped kennel and double-security fencing.

There should be indoor/outdoor runs for exercise, and a good brand of food should be fed. It's a bonus to have your pet bathed and "de-bugged" before his return home. Check with your vet whether Houdini needs any booster shots; good boarding kennels require them.

When you drop him off at his home away from home, you should leave the name of Houdini's vet, with any special instructions. If you wish, leave Houdini a reminder of home, a favorite toy or a security blanket. Carry it next to your body for a day to give it your own "eau de cologne." A few owners actually tape their voice or send letters for their pet!

Some boarding kennels are canine Hiltons, offering your dog luxuries such as brass beds, classical music, and gourmet foods made of chicken and liver pâtés. You may be the one to receive a postcard from your dog, saying, "Wish you were here," or "Don't hurry home."

I'd like to take Angel along. Can she stay with me in a motel/hotel/campgrounds, or the like?

You need to do some advance planning. Families who rent cabins or campsites should inquire beforehand whether dogs are allowed, as should those staying at motels, hotels, or lodges. Some vacation areas welcome dogs; however, irresponsible dog owners have caused pets to be banned at places that have been left dogeared. Ask about necessary immunizations or health papers, especially if you'll be crossing national borders.

When you pack for yourself, include a suitcase for Angel too, with leash, brush, medications, favorite toys, and a couple of bowls. Stow her food and take enough water to acclimate her slowly to the water of the area. Include a container of Kaopectate in case of Montezuma's revenge, for dog or owner. Attach her tags to her collar as an ID.

Take a crate unless you will be with your pet at all times. Even an Angel can turn to a bit of deviltry if she is "abandoned" in strange quarters. Crating Angel also prevents her accidental escape from a room. Ask the manager where you may exercise her, and offer to make a deposit against any damage that may occur despite your diligence. Keep her on leash in public, and do not invade swimming or eating areas. Not everybody appreciates the heavenly attributes of your pet.

My old dog gets upset when he's not at home. Because of his age, I don't want to change his routine. What about dog sitters?

When it comes to dog sitters, you have several choices. You can ask a relative or friend to take your pet into his home if both parties are comfortable with that idea, possibly on a reciprocal agreement. They watch your two Clumber Spaniels and goldfish in July, and you watch their python in August. If you don't think that's an even swap, you can arrange for someone to go to your home. A dog sitter may stop by to perform chores, or she may stay in your home. If you are hiring a stranger, you should ask for references; you may also want to ask her to meet your dog and become familiar with your routine beforehand.

Whether you choose a kennel or a dog sitter, leave complete instructions, any medications, plenty of food, the veterinary clinic number, and an emergency phone where you may be reached.

We're moving to another state. I've been thinking about shipping Gulliver by air. What will I need?

If you don't already have an airline shipping crate, buy one so that Gulliver can become accustomed to it. Within ten days of his flight, take him to your vet for a checkup and for the health certificate required by all airlines. Tranquilizing animals before shipping is *not* generally recommended and should be done only under veterinarian prescription.

Reservations should be made at least one day in advance. Avoid weekends, torrid and freezing temperatures, or peak traffic periods. Try to book a direct flight, or at least one in which Gulliver will not have to change planes. Withhold food and limit water for twelve hours before shipping. Line the crate with shredded paper for Gulliver's comfort and for absorbing any possible accidents due to stress. Arrive an hour or two early, as baggage is loaded before passengers, and walk him one more time just before leaving him. The address and phone number of the recipient must accompany your dog, so be prepared to relate this information. You may also purchase insurance for your pet. Write his name on the crate, so personnel can call him by name and calm him if necessary. If you are on the same flight, you may ask the attendant to check on your dog in baggage.

The airline staff can inform you of other regulations or special instructions for a lengthy flight. Although employees are not supposed to open the crate, exceptions may be made in case of delay or emergency. Attach a small bowl to the inside of the door so that Gulliver may be fed or watered, if necessary, without opening the crate.

Be sure you, or somebody, is at the other end of the flight to receive your pet. He should be taken for a walk immediately and spoiled a bit. Some dogs are frightened by the experience, and others take to flying with aplomb, sprouting their wings like the mythical Pegasus.

Can Molly accompany me on my cruise?

No U.S. ships allow pets aboard. Noah had animals on board, but because he didn't provide shuffleboard and rumba lessons, the Ark didn't have much of a party atmosphere anyway. Pair by pair, the animals moped below deck, causing a heck of a disposal problem for the crew. Pets were on the *Titanic* too, but most met the same fate as their masters.

Leave Molly on dry land, enjoy yourself, and, when you return, take her for a rowboat ride.

Can Ming Ling come with me while I'm backpacking through Europe?

Many countries have restrictions concerning dogs, and several have quarantines. Some of these quarantines are expensive and are so lengthy it is impractical to take your dog into another country unless you are changing residence. For instance, the United Kingdom has a six-month quarantine, as do Ireland, Barbados, and Hong Kong. Even Hawaii quarantines for three months. New Zealand and Australia require nine months, and certain areas of the world do not allow *any* dogs from North America within their borders! On the other hand, Canada and most of continental Europe have no quarantine.

Health certificate demands also vary from only rabies to distemper, hepatitis, leptospirosis, parvovirus, kennel cough, and heartworm tests, as well as rabies. Each country is different, so check on requirements *before* you load Ming Ling's backpack.

Europeans generally welcome well-mannered dogs anywhere—

cafés, parks, or stores. You should realize, however, that you may limit your acceptance into certain areas if you are accompanied by a dog, as well as committing yourself to obligations to your pet. It's not easy to climb mountains with a Pekingese!

I've seen a seat belt for dogs advertised. Is this really necessary?

Dogs are often hurt in car accidents, and a seat belt helps prevent injuries. Look for a product such as Saf-T Car Harness or Buckle Up. A crate can also be protective. One of the worst problems for dogs involved in accidents is the terror they suffer. If they become loose, the fear causes flight, and, even if injuries are minor, your dog may be lost to you forever.

Why can't Shep just ride in the back of my truck? That's what being a dog is all about.

The *most* dangerous way for a dog to travel is in the back of a pickup. Falling out, being thrown from the truck bed, jumping in front of another vehicle, and being hit all add to severe trauma and fatality statistics. Products such as the Saf-T Truck Harness are made to keep Shep safe in the truck while allowing him to lie down, stand, or move about.

Every time we go anywhere Pepper gets carsick. Any suggestions?

Start by simply placing her in the car, with the doors open, petting and talking to her. As she relaxes, give her a special treat and let her experience the car as a pleasant place to be. Next time, start the engine but don't move the car. Eventually, you can slowly back out of the driveway and then take short spins around the block, all while Pepper has an empty stomach. Eventually she will become a cross-country traveler.

Be sure your pup's trips are not always as upsetting as sour apples, that is, leaving her brothers and sisters, going to the vet's for shots, taking a trip to the boarding kennel. Plan a short romp after each excursion, so car rides become positive experiences.

If she continues being carsick, change her riding habits. Place her in a crate, filled with plenty of shredded paper. Try to position her so she does not see the road and cows flying by. Flying cows are enough to make anyone sick. If none of these attempts is curative, talk to your vet about the possibility of anti-motion-sickness medication to use before you start on long trips.

I like to take Jinx with me, but I'd just die if anything happened to him. What if he gets lost?

First, if your dog is "misplaced," keep your attitude positive to help calm yourself. If you've taken preventive measures such as attaching a tag to his collar, having him tattooed, and teaching him to come when you call, you've got a good chance of finding him. You should also have pictures of Jinx, both groomed and "au natural," to use on posters and to show people.

Alarms draw attention; spread the news. Tell the mail carrier, neighbors, and everyone you see. Phone the police, veterinary hospitals, and animal control organizations. Call schools and ask them to make an announcement. Visit—calling is not enough—shelters and ask to see the animals.

Sherlock Bones, professional dog finder, suggests placing an ad on the radio and in the newspaper, offering a reward of one hundred to three hundred dollars. This amount makes it worthwhile for people to join the search. A lesser figure won't make a dognapper endanger himself when he can sell Jinx for as much money to others, and a reward of more than three hundred dollars can be a tipoff of value, inviting extortion.

Have posters printed and plaster the vicinity of the loss. Go door to door, showing the poster and asking people to call you. Have someone stay by your phone so that callers don't become tired of attempting to reach you unsuccessfully. Local dog club members are often willing to help by manning a phone, checking pounds, and so on. Call them; they're all dog lovers!

While you're away or sleeping (if that's possible), leave a bowl of his favorite food in an open crate, kennel, or garage. Place an item of clothing bearing your scent nearby. If Jinx finds his way home, he'll have reason to stay even if you aren't there to greet him.

If these measures don't work, ask authorities whether you can put a humane trap (a crate that is baited with food and automatically closes) in the area of his last sighting. Don't give up hope. Keep looking and continue calling his name. When the lost dog is a male, you can appeal to his romantic nature with a bitch in season. Both sexes respond to others of their kind when they are too panicked to approach even a much-loved human. Some gung-ho gun dogs are drawn to the sound of a shot being fired, music to their ears and an alert to their hunting instincts.

On the other hand, what if I find a lost dog?

Remember how you'd feel if it were your pet. If the dog has a tag, notify the local animal shelter or dog control office. Call radio stations and the newspaper, asking them to announce the find. Many offer this service without charge. Describe the dog to area veterinarians; they may have a dog fitting the description among their clientele. As mentioned before, spread the word to other people who can activate the grapevine.

How long do the pounds keep a found dog?

Time limits depend on the organization, no matter what its name: the pound, humane society, animal rescue association, or pet control. Some make a lifetime commitment, and, once the animal is harbored within its doors, it is kept until a new home is found or until it dies of natural causes. Of course, budget and space can only stretch so far and, when they are filled, there is no room at the inn until a current resident moves on.

Others range from a minimal three days to a week or longer before offering the dog for adoption. Cute, healthy, friendly purebred animals have the best chances of finding new homes. Check with all local organizations daily, or better yet, twice daily, in person, to see whether your dog has been found. Many animal control officers just wouldn't know a Briard or a Sealyham Terrier if there were a $1 million reward for its return. Dirty, scruffy, and thin, your pet can be confused with anything, even if it's a well-known breed.

When an unwanted animal is adopted from one of these organizations, neutering or spaying is required, as well as inoculations. Purina

Dogfoods now offers a plan allowing senior citizens to adopt new friends from shelters, covering adoption and initial veterinary expenses.

Can dogs really find their way home?

Stories of dogs trekking their way home, sometimes over amazing distances and occasionally after lengthy periods, are not unusual. Tales such as *The Incredible Journey* and *Lassie Come Home* demonstrate this ability. Possibly they find their way through their superior sense of smell or through recall of familiar territory. Or perhaps it is the call of rapture they know will greet them on their return. Some dogs have an unbelievable ability to orient themselves to the environment through familiar objects. They have compasses for brains. It is not wise to rely totally on their instincts, however, if you've lost your buddy.

What good is tattooing?

Although dogs can't pick the word *Mother* or portray an eagle or an anchor to decorate their biceps, a number tattooed discreetly inside an upper hind leg can save its life or turn the lost into the found. Many dog clubs and veterinarians offer this service. The flank is clipped, cleaned, and numbed, with the owner's Social Security number then painlessly tattooed on the left or the AKC registration on the right. This tattoo may then be listed with an organization such as National Dog Registry (NDR). A fee is paid for each listed number and covers every dog bearing it. NDR has 24-hour, 365-day-a-year phone service. Working with this organization can unite a dog with its owner in a short period. The AKC number is, of course, already listed with that club.

Legally, no dog with a tattoo may be used by a research laboratory. This protects lost or stolen pets. Sadly, many animals are stolen in an attempt to make money from selling "hot" dogs to labs. Animals that are not marked turn a quick profit for dognappers. Tattooed ears are usually mutilated before dogs reach their doom.

Tattooing is a quick, painless, inexpensive method of legal identification and protection for your dog.

13
The Dating Game

Is it a good idea to neuter my pup? How old should she be?

Neutering (spaying the female or castrating the male) is the best way to avoid frustration—your pet's and yours. Neutering eliminates the peskiness of the heat cycle, the annoyance of a lusty male, and fights between testy parties of the same sex. These surgeries also prevent cancers and infections of the reproductive organs. Especially if done at the onset of puberty, spaying can nearly eliminate the risk of breast tumors as well. At this optimum time of canine adolescence, growth is essentially complete, and masculine or feminine attributes are already apparent, so surgery has no adverse effect on these characteristics.

Puberty arrives when a male begins lifting his leg or a female approaches her first season, at *about* one year of age. Small breeds frequently mature much earlier, large breeds somewhat later. Ask the breeder of your pup to suggest a good age or follow your veterinarian's advice. It's never too late, however. If you decide to neuter your three-year-old (or even eight-year-old) dog, the surgery still has benefits.

Is neutering surgery hard on them? I've heard it makes them fat.

Dogs recuperate quickly from neutering surgery, particularly at a young age. If you wait until a raging uterine infection or repeated cesareans force you to spay, she will take longer to feel perky again.

Only owners make dogs fat. If you continue exercising her and adjusting her diet according to her waistline, she'll continue being her svelte self. As she ages, she'll need less food since she'll be burning fewer calories than in her youth.

Aren't we taking away their rights of reproduction?

Rights? Her right to develop pyometra, mastitis, milk fever, or uterine cancer and to suffer the pain of multiple births or cesarean sections? His right to be frustrated, to develop testicular cancer, to wander to his ladylove and be hit by a car or shot by an irate "in-law"? Your right to deal with hostile phone calls, pay the vet bills, fight off males from your doorstep, mop the floor daily to cleanse the mess made by her season, and to worry?

Her right to have pups, only to have them taken away weeks later; his right to be a noncustodial father; and your right to care for puppies hours each day?

Dogs only have the rights their owners give them, and we can give them the right to a peaceful, healthy nonparental life.

Right?

What if Tootsie is accidentally bred?

Sometimes 1 + 1 = 12 and, if that's not in your budget or plans, you can take immediate steps to change those figures. Your vet can give Tootsie a "mismating" shot so that the fertilized eggs will not attach to the uterine lining. This must be done within forty-eight hours of the dastardly deed—the sooner, the better. A better-late-than-never alternative would be to spay Tootsie within the first two weeks of pregnancy. Up to that time, there is little change in the uterus.

To avoid an unplanned pregnancy, you can talk to the vet about "birth control pills," which halt or postpone her season. If you ever plan to breed Tootsie, however, you cannot spay her, and meddling with nature by using abortion shots or birth control pills is not advised.

To reduce the chance of a mistake, confine your bitch during her season, walk her on leash, and keep a strict parental eye on her every second she is outdoors. But the best way to prevent unwanted puppies is still to neuter.

Nacho tries to breed everything in sight—males, females, dogs, humans, guests, chairs. It's embarrassing! Will it help if I can find him a girlfriend?

No, it will make him worse. Although he seems to have a poor choice in mates, his taste of forbidden fruit will only spur him on to more conquests. If Nacho's place is by your side—not on your leg— you can curb those urges by having him neutered.

If Nacho's future is as a showman, however, you don't have that option and must resort to distracting him with toys or long walks—or put up with a macho Nacho. If you're tired of being the object of his affection, you can buy more chairs or plan a large dinner party.

When will Kandy come into season for the first time?

When you buy your female pup, ask the breeder what age Kandy's dam was when she had her first season. Reproductive cycling and breeding tendencies of daughters often follow those of their mothers. The first season may be as early as six months or as late as two years, depending on the breed and bloodline. From then on, dogs normally cycle on a regular schedule, about every six months.

Is breeding dogs worthwhile?

In hourly wages, never. If you count your payment in puppy kisses, maybe. Breeders must pay for a prenatal exam (including X rays and tests), stud fee, extra food, whelping equipment, paperwork, registration, advertising, presale checkups, worming, and inoculations. In addition, they may have the expense of shipping or traveling, a cesarean section, ear cropping, tail docking, dewclaw removal, and additional medical attention. You're lucky to break even, and any profit is taxable.

Breeders worry about the dam's and the puppies' well-being, because either or both sometimes have serious health problems or even die. Birth deformities and the problems of finding good homes

and fulfilling guarantees are also concerns. Sometimes puppies are returned; buyers are disgruntled, disappointed, or worried; or a litter becomes critically ill. News of puppies' being killed by a car or having hemophilia, hip dysplasia, cataracts, or any congenital defect is agonizing to the breeder who cuddled and loved them. Only you can decide whether you feel the result compensates for the work and problems involved.

If I do decide to breed Sophie, how old should she be?

The ideal time for a first litter is when Sophie is between eighteen months and three years of age. Vets recommend waiting until the second or third heat cycle, when the prospective dam reaches physical and mental maturity. Professional breeders have found that bitches produce larger and more robust litters when bred only once a year.

Where do I find a stud? Why is the range of stud fees so wide?

Studs are advertised in breed magazines, giving you the choice of Champions, prospective Champions, or obedience titleholders—all dogs with high-quality pedigrees. Sometimes vets can give you suggestions, particularly if you have a populous breed. They know which dogs are producing vigorous, healthy, attractive pups.

Stud fees vary according to the breed, titles, the dog's demand, the owner's reputation, and the quality of progeny. This is no time to skimp. If your bitch is good enough to breed, you'll want the best for her. Pinching pennies shows up in the puppies.

What if I pay a stud fee and Ari doesn't have pups?

Before breeding Ari, you should ask the stud owner whether you have the option of a return service in case of a *miss*, as it's called. Many stud owners guarantee a live litter with a minimum number of pups. The timing can be off, and it's possible she can conceive the following season. Help ensure that by choosing a *proven* sire (one that has already produced live puppies) and asking your vet to check vaginal smears microscopically to see which day of her season is best for conception.

What exactly are linebreeding/outcrossing/inbreeding/ crossbreeding?

The closer the breeding, the more likely the end product will mirror its ancestors. In breeder terminology, *inbreeding* means mating mother/ son, father/daughter, or brother/sister. The term *linebreeding* is given to matings that have a common relative: parent, grandparent, or another ancestor. When a breeding takes place between two totally unrelated dogs, it is termed an *outcross*, the most extreme of which is a *crossbreeding* (between two different breeds).

Most professionals use linebreeding as their basis, with an occasional outcross or inbreeding to pick up or set in an attribute. Recommended reading on these subjects, genetics and breeding, is listed in Suggested Reading (see pp. 191–92).

Before I breed Tory, should I do anything special?

You don't want to jeopardize Tory or her pups by breeding her in anything but superb condition, so schedule an appointment at your veterinary clinic a month or so before she is due in season. The vet will test a stool sample, update her shots, perform a pelvic exam, and check her for any hereditary abnormalities. The stud owner may require or the vet suggest various additional tests: canine brucellosis, culture, heartworm (if not already done), for example.

Choose your stud and call his owner on the first day of season for a reservation. Make sure Tory is at a good lean weight and in tip-top shape.

Do you think it helps to have the stud mate her more than once?

It takes only one breeding for fertilization, but timing must be right. This is why it is safest, particularly for a maiden bitch, to be bred once and then again at a return engagement forty-eight hours later.

Sampson is six months old. I'd like to cash in on this breeding game. So what do I do?

Males must be at least seven months at the time of breeding and no more than twelve years old, or the AKC requires an affidavit proving paternity. To ask and receive stud fees large enough to compensate for your time and trouble (more about that later), Sampson must be registered, proven, of sterling pedigree, and certified free of hereditary defects. Usually he has achieved wins and/or titles in the show ring. If you have a dog with these assets, you can advertise him and his virtues in breed magazines.

When you are contacted, you should make sure the female is of good quality. If anything goes wrong with the pups, Sampson will receive the blame, just like the old "my kids when they're good, your kids when they're bad" routine.

Experienced stud owners can tell you it's no picnic. Breeders wear a path to the airport picking up bitches who are not at all happy about being away from home, sitting in a stuffy plane or car for hours, and having their "privates" examined by strangers. In short, these females can be downright bitchy. Sometimes they don't like you, or they don't like the stud, or they like the wrong male. It isn't just nature taking its course. If you're taking money for breedings, you must be willing and able to restrain a reluctant female and aid an untried male.

Between gas for airport trips, food for the visiting lady, periodic veterinary examinations, a safety kennel (100 percent dogproof), layoff periods when your stud picks up a bug, and hospitality for the "in-laws," the stud fee pays starvation hourly wages. By the time you deduct purchase price and show and advertising costs from any profit, there's just enough to make the IRS look askance at your "breeding game." To cap everything, after his first taste of love, Sampson howls his desire to the world every time a bitch is in season within three miles.

I've heard of something called leasing. What is that?

Leasing can be the answer when you want to breed to a particular stud and don't have a suitable female. It can bring in another bloodline or allow you to prove your own female's young son without inbreeding.

The advantages of leasing are numerous. The bitch doesn't take up permanent residence but is only an extended house guest until she has her litter. Although leasing isn't cheap, it's less expensive than purchasing a bitch with outstanding attributes you wish to add to your lines.

Of course, leasing a bitch is much like needing money to make money. Unless you know the circles to pass the word, it's difficult to find or be approved for the opportunity. There's no Rent-a-Bitch listing in the yellow pages.

What is the oldest age at which a dog can be bred? I'd like to keep one of old Star's pups.

The American Kennel Club only registers litters out of dams over eight months and under twelve years. Anything younger or older is beyond reasonable limits when considering Star's health. In addition, as dams age, they often become less fertile, producing fewer—sometimes no—pups.

If you want to keep one of Star's twinkles, it's best to choose one by the time she's five, or you may miss her chance to keep shining.

I've seen dogs "stuck" together. What is this?

The *tie* is a natural phenomenon of dogs. If you intend to breed professionally, books on the subject can give you the logistics of how and why. The tie takes place during ejaculation and is conducive to conception, although not necessary. Most ties last ten to twenty minutes, although they can range from none at all to over an hour. They will end only when they end, and any human intervention to halt and desist will only cause injury to both dogs.

I have a little male and a big female. They couldn't have puppies, could they?

How recently have you checked?

Anything is possible in the game of love. Little would-be studs climb on chairs or on the bitch herself, and a shameless female co-operates in every way possible, scrunching down to his level if need be. Matings have been accomplished through chain-link fences, by climbing over gates and crashing through doors or windows. The reverse situation is also possible; owners should be aware that the combination of a large stud and small female often creates insurmountable complications in whelping.

Don't take any chances. Securely confine one or both dogs during heat cycles. But remember: the only sure birth control is neutering.

Joy gained weight and looked as if she were going to have puppies, but she didn't. What happened?

Mother Nature sometimes plays jokes on female dogs and their owners. After a season, a bitch can develop a condition commonly termed "false" pregnancy, whether savvy brood matron or innocent maiden. In cooperation with an overload of maternal hormones, these wishful mothers swell, develop milk, nest, and exhibit other symptoms of a normal pregnancy that disappear like a will-o'-the-wisp. If this becomes a habit each season, you should make a decision about whether to breed Joy or spay her, to ensure her health and comfort and to end frustrations for both of you.

Do I really need a fancy whelping box? Where should I plan for Kara to have her family?

Fancy isn't necessary—Kara would be perfectly content with the middle of your bed or the back of your closet. To forestall such poor choices, supply her with a box large enough for her and her family. Line the box with several layers of newspaper and have an old blanket or a piece of washable carpet ready after the litter's arrival. Convincing the little mother of the advantages of her box over your bed may take some pretty-please persuading.

Place Kara's box in an out-of-the-way, but convenient spot. She'll need peace and quiet, but you'll want to poke your head in to check on her delivery progress and later to ooooooooooh and awwwwwwwwwww over the pups a hundred times a day. A spare room or a corner of your garage or basement is ideal—as long as it is warm, dry, and clean—a good place for bringing up a family. Litters do "litter," so it's best to pick a place easy to clean and deodorize.

Dogs are natural mothers, aren't they? I wouldn't want to help deliver the pups.

Canines possess an abundance of instincts, but problems can and do occur. And maybe your bitch is a natural hunter, but was "behind the door" when whelping instinct was handed out. Even if she's had pups previously with no difficulty, this time a pup could be wedged in the wrong position and block delivery.

Don't breed your bitch unless you're prepared to serve as a midwife and to assist her or to obtain help if necessary. Anything less could be a fatal decision for your bitch and her pups.

What should I do if Trixie won't or can't feed her puppies?

Your veterinarian or a professional breeder can tell you how and when to tube- or bottle-feed the babes should the need arise. Whichever method you choose, you must take Trixie's place in providing formula, feeding several times a day and adjusting amounts. And if Trixie can't care for the pups, you'll also have to take over bathroom chores as well; you'll have to clean and massage their genitals to help them urinate and defecate, functions they cannot perform by themselves for the first two weeks or so of life. While you're cleaning and drying the pups, you can give them the cuddling and affection their four-legged mother can't provide.

These problems are part of the canine facts of life. If you cannot face them or carry them out as foster mother, Trixie's puppies will die. No excuses accepted.

How do I go about selling Dawn's pups? How can I make sure they'll all get good homes?

Planning a litter of puppies is not the same as planning a family. No breeder intends to keep an entire litter; nor can he afford to spend the money, time, or kennel space necessary to keep them even if he wants to. But will anyone care for them the way you do?

Examine ads that capture your interest and pattern yours after them, using a catchy, attention-getting phrase. Determine a fair price and stick to it. Cut-rate prices attract cut-rate buyers. Advertising in the newspaper and dog magazines, a notice in your vet clinic, and passing the news by word-of-mouth should bring plenty of callers. Your job is to sort through the prospects and find good owners for Dawn's pups.

Remember the kennels you visited years ago when looking for Dawn; you're now in the reverse position. Many of the things you looked for in a seller can be applied to buyers: cleanliness, interest in responsible care, a loving caress, a rapport between pup and person.

Ask the potential buyers whether this is their first dog and why they decided to buy one now. If they've had another dog, find out what happened to it. These questions can be covered through normal conversation, so that it doesn't seem you are giving them the third degree. Determine how they plan to house and exercise their new pup. You don't want her squashed on the highway after all Dawn's and your hard work.

Make certain the buyers realize all the requirements of your particular breed—grooming, feeding, exercising, socializing. Introduce them to the mother, so they can picture their adorable, cuddly bundle in the future with adult looks, size, and temperament.

Recommend a training class and books on your breed. Suggest neutering all pets for their health and the owner's convenience. Ask them to notify you later if they can't keep the dog for any reason. Don't misrepresent the pup or the breed; if you do, the buyers will be unhappy with their purchase. Then everyone suffers, especially the pup.

Don't be afraid you'll lose a sale by asking questions. It's a big job and you've got to do it. There's a living being depending on you.

When each pup is sent on its way, you will have mixed emotions as you wave good-bye. You've become attached, and you'll miss each one. You're the proud "parent," and you've done your best by them, including locating a solid, loving future. It's time they go to their own homes. Your life will go back to its normal routine, and your work detail will be less.

It's sort of like sending the grandchildren home.

14
The Show Must Go On

Why do people want to show their dogs?

Since time immemorial, people have enjoyed the thrill of competition. We love to crow, "My Tyrannosaurus runs faster than your Triceratops," or "My dad makes more money than your dad," or "My dog's better than your dog."

Dog shows are a sport and hobby for competitive individuals, just like golfing, bowling, and horse racing. They are also a breeder's showcase. Professional breeders, who are driven by their goals for improving the breed and producing the dog closest to the ideal, are able to show off their successes, or see where they need to improve. They increase sales by enhancing their reputations with show wins.

When did dog shows get started?

The first recorded event was held in Newcastle, England, in 1859. At the same time, interest was growing on the other side of the ocean. In 1877, the first Westminster Kennel Club show was held in New York City, making it the second oldest continuous sporting event in the United States (the first being the Kentucky Derby).

Even before that time, around 1700, the craftspeople in Flanders brushed up their dogs, clasped a hand-designed collar around their pets' necks, and paraded them on every other Sunday. In fact, the guild workmen offered an "exhibition" for Schipperkes in 1690.

The early show enthusiasts didn't just hop into their vans and travel for an hour to a cluster of shows. Each event lasted four or five days and was reached via a long, tiring, dirty ride by railroad or horse-drawn wagon. Hired kennel managers not only bred and trained the dogs, but took them to the shows and exhibited them. Today, although some dogs are shown by professionals, shows are often a family affair.

What exactly are obedience and conformation?

Obedience competition involves teaching the dog to obey on command, with each class requiring progressively more difficult exercises. *Conformation* (or *breed*) judging determines which dog most closely conforms to the ideal described in the breed Standard. Obedience allows showing of neutered animals, but conformation competitors must be intact.

Many spectators find obedience more interesting to observe. If the dog performs well and follows commands, it is apparent to most onlookers.

Conformation judging is harder to follow, much like an Agatha Christie mystery. Who will it be? The judge peers in the dog's mouth, checks size and coat, observes structure and other intricacies, and also requires the animal to show its gait. The breed ring may appear to be more arbitrary because the judge is giving her personal opinion, unlike the obedience official, who scores according to explicit requirements. Although the entry that best represents the breed should be the object of the search, one judge may find a noble head appealing. Another is struck by breathtaking movement, and a weekday dentist/weekend judge looks for complete dentition and a correct bite.

Can I show Bingo in both?

Some owners believe you cannot simultaneously train a dog in both obedience and conformation. Their theory is that the dog may sit when it should stand, or that heeling will ruin the sparkling showmanship admired in the breed ring.

This is a fallacy, because a dog can be taught to do anything within its physical and mental capabilities, whether walking at heel precisely on cue or hitting the end of the lead to fly around the ring when told. Many owners, however, are only interested in one arena of competition. Training is time-consuming, and even those owners who wish dual titles for their dogs often concentrate on one challenge at a time. If you have the time and energy to train and show Bingo in both, however, there is no reason why you can't accomplish this feat concurrently.

How much does this cost? Will I win $$$$$?

During the 1980s, show entry fees averaged fourteen to twenty dollars per show, per dog. Although these fees seem reasonable enough, your budget must stretch to include the necessary supplies, gas to reach the site, and possibly rooming or meals. At the show, you'll want to buy a catalog that lists the competition, a cute kid will hit you up for a raffle ticket, and your husband will see a Borzoi tie tack he just has to have because it looks just like Poochie. Soon your daughter wants a dog of her own to show, and then you have to trade the station wagon for a van to haul them.

All the various accouterments collected slowly for Poochie—training classes, crate, leash, and several collars to grow into—must be paid for immediately after Czarina's purchase so you can begin showing her. You decide they can share the grooming equipment, because you can only brush one at a time anyway, but it's time you bought a grooming table and a tack box to carry the brushes, sprays, and combs. You fence the yard and erect kennel runs, so Czarina and Poochie can run and build up muscle. Entry costs double, but gas and lodging stay the same, so you figure it's a bargain: twice the fun for only a few more dollars.

One day you realize Poochie shines in obedience, and Czarina finishes her Championship, so you breed her to the best stud you can find, and, of course, you keep one of the pups. So now you must add another kennel, buy an RV to travel in, and you're looking seriously at six acres outside the city limits. You realize you're hooked.

Cash prizes are seldom offered, and, when they are, rarely do they cover the expenses incurred. But you have won countless friends; you've got an exciting hobby and a roomful of trophies. And, if that's not enough, you've got Poochie, Czarina, and Nicholas the Great.

I heard somebody at my obedience class talking about needing three legs. I thought all dogs needed four!

Qualifying obedience scores are called *legs*. Because three qualifications are required for each title, an obedience dog has seven legs, four given to him at birth and three more earned by his prowess. The dog who has gained all three titles, therefore, has thirteen legs.

Doesn't training place restrictions on dogs? Shouldn't they just be allowed to be themselves?

Dogs in training can still enjoy the benefits of their ilk—chewing on a meaty bone, curling up by your feet, chasing a ball, and walking with their favorite people. In fact, just like well-behaved children, trained dogs are welcome in more places and are able to accompany their owners more often. Although children have to be allowed to experience the wonderful world of being kids, they must attend school, learn to behave, and recognize certain rules and requirements. This doesn't restrict their activity (although they may argue differently) but actually enhances it, as they learn when they grow up.

Like teenagers, dogs may sigh or moan, but they're not always able to be on their own. They're actually happier when someone in authority sets the parameters and acts as a loving leader of the pack.

How old does Wendy have to be?

Although she can be trained at a younger age, Wendy must be at least six months old on the day of the show for both licensed Obedience and Conformation competition. There are no upper age limits, and shows may offer Veteran classes for dogs over seven or eight years of age. Ironically, the puppy and Veteran classes, the alpha and omega at shows, are always spectator favorites.

Matches, at which entrants may be as young as two to four months, are often hosted by clubs. These provide wonderful training for novice handlers and dogs and are great fun for exhibitors, judges, spectators, and canines alike.

How do I go about finding shows and entering them?

Several dog magazines list shows with their dates and locations. You can also contact local clubs and superintendents (see Helpful Addresses, pp. 187–90) to ask about area events. It is best to attend a show or participate in a match before trying to conquer the world of point shows. Study entry forms (premium lists) obtained from the superintendents, noting the necessary fees and the dates of entry closing.

Fill in the blanks, writing legibly. On the AKC form, spaces are available for the following:

Breed
Variety (if appropriate)[1]
Sex
Dog show class
Class division (if appropriate)[2]
Additional classes[3]

[1]Breeds with varieties are Cocker Spaniels, Dachshunds, Collies, Bull Terriers, Manchester Terriers, Chihuahuas, English Toy Spaniels, and Poodles.
[2]Consult the classification for your breed to see whether there is a division for color, weight, or puppies' age.
[3]You may enter your dog in more than one class if he is eligible, but, if he is beaten in any class, he may not compete for Championship points.

Obedience trial class (if appropriate)
Junior showmanship class (if appropriate)
Name of junior handler (if appropriate)
Full name of dog (must be registered name)
Identifying number of dog
Date of birth
Place (country) of birth
Breeder's name
Sire's name
Dam's name
Owner's name
Owner's address
Owner's agent (handler, if appropriate)
Your signature
Telephone number

CKC shows are entered in the same manner as AKC, except that all entries must be identified by either tattoo or noseprint (similar to a fingerprint).

UKC requires a copy of the registration certificate for show entries, along with a pedigree for conformation shows.

What classes are there?

Your choices in obedience are Novice A or B, Open A or B, Utility, and Tracking. With the exception of Tracking, which may be taken at any point, progress is consecutive, beginning with Novice. After receipt of the Novice title (CD), you and your dog may compete in Open. Utility is the highest class.

Novice A is for handlers who have not previously owned or co-owned a dog with an obedience title (even if they did not handle the animal themselves). Any owner and dog (without a CD) may enter Novice B. Open A is for entrants that have not completed a CDX title, and Open B is for those that have the title, because they may continue showing in this class for trophies and for points (explained later). Utility may be broken into A and B at large shows but is usually offered as one class to dogs with or without the Utility title. *Note:* A bitch in season may not be shown in Obedience.

Conformation classes include Puppy (which may be divided into six to nine months and nine to twelve months), Novice, Bred-by-Ex-

OFFICIAL AMERICAN KENNEL CLUB ENTRY FORM

PUPPY LUV KENNEL CLUB

Date: 1/1/91

I ENCLOSE $ . . . . 15 . . . for entry fees

IMPORTANT—Read Carefully Instructions on Reverse Side Before Filling Out. Numbers in the boxes indicate sections of the instructions relevant to the information needed in that box (PLEASE PRINT)

BREED Bearded Collie	VARIETY 1		SEX M

DOG [2] [3] SHOW CLASS BOB	CLASS ☐ DIVISION Weight color etc

ADDITIONAL CLASSES Open B	OBEDIENCE TRIAL CLASS Utility	JR SHOWMANSHIP CLASS Novice Junior

NAME OF (See Back) JUNIOR HANDLER (if any) Lauryn Viernow

FULL NAME OF DOG **CH WALKOWAY'S MILLION DOLLAR WIN UD**

Enter number here

✗	AKC REG NO X1111111 AKC LITTER NO	DATE OF BIRTH 12/31/89
☐	ILP NO FOREIGN REG NO & COUNTRY	PLACE OF ☒USA ☐ Canada ☐ Foreign BIRTH Do not print the above in catalog

BREEDER **Chris & Ed Walkowicz**

SIRE **CH Megabucks' Big Daddy CDX**

DAM **CH/OTCH Walkoway's Million Dollar Dream**

ACTUAL OWNER(S) Lauryn Viernow [4] (Please Print) RR 1 OWNER'S ADDRESS CITY Somewhere, STATE IL ZIP 60000

NAME OF OWNERS AGENT (IF ANY) AT THE SHOW **Chris Walkowicz**

I CERTIFY that I am the actual owner of the dog, or that I am the duly authorized agent of the actual owner whose name I have entered above. In consideration of the acceptance of this entry, I (we) agree to abide by the rules and regulations of The American Kennel Club in effect at the time of this show or obedience trial, and by any additional rules and regulations appearing in the premium list for this show or obedience trial or both, and further agree to be bound by the "Agreement" printed on the reverse side of this entry form. I (we) certify and represent that the dog entered is not a hazard to persons or other dogs. This entry is submitted for acceptance on the foregoing representation and agreement.

SIGNATURE of owner or his agent duly authorized to make this entry

TELEPHONE #

hibitor, American Bred, and Open, all separated by sex. Best of Breed is offered only for Champions of Record.

Ages for puppy classes are determined as of the show date; that is, if your puppy is nine months old on June 15, and the show is held that day, he must be entered in nine to twelve months. If the show is on June 14, the proper class is six to nine months. Specialty (one-breed) shows may also offer a twelve- to eighteen-month class. Novice is for any dog that has not won three blue ribbons prior to the closing date of entries. Entries in the Bred-by-Exhibitor classes must be bred and handled by the owner. American Bred is only for dogs bred and whelped in this country, and Open—as the name signifies—is open to all, including those eligible for all other classes. Imports (dogs bred in other countries) may only be shown in Puppy, Open, and Best of Breed classes.

I've entered Beowulf at a show. How will I know what to do so I won't look like an amateur?

Plan to arrive at the show site early. When you have taken care of vital necessities, find your ring and watch the judge's technique. Ask the steward assisting the judge whether breeds are on time as listed. (They cannot be held earlier than scheduled but may be a bit late.) Have Beowulf groomed, slick up yourself, and allow plenty of time to be at ringside early.

As the steward calls your class, enter the ring and pose Beowulf. Occasionally, the judge will ask you to walk or run the dog around first. Follow the judge's instructions, and don't be afraid to ask him to explain if you are unsure. If you do goof, don't be embarrassed. All handlers were novices once, and even the pros make mistakes.

After the class is judged, four ribbons may be given for placings. If you've received one, thank the judge and leave the ring. The first-place dog must return to the ring for Winners competition with all other blue-ribbon holders. The dog judged best among these receives the Championship point(s). The second-place dog from the winner's class (whether Puppy, Open, or whatever) then reenters the ring, and a Reserve Winner is also picked in case the Winners Dog or Bitch should be found ineligible for any reason. This is rare, but it does sometimes happen, so it's worthwhile to stay for the class!

Winners Dog and Winners Bitch continue competing with the Champions in the Best of Breed (sometimes called *specials*) class.

A Best of Breed (BOB) and Best of Opposite Sex (BOS) are chosen. All BOBs may then compete in Group judging, and the first place in each group knock heads for the prestigious Best in Show (BIS) award. In other words, you continue competing with Beowulf until he is beaten.

What are specialty shows?

Specialty shows are held for one breed only, as opposed to all-breed shows, which are open to all recognized breeds. Obedience trials may be held separately or in conjunction with specialty or all-breed shows.

What will I need to show Dixie?

The only equipment absolutely vital to show your dog is a leash with a collar, appropriate to the ring and breed. It is likely you'll want to give Dixie a quick brush, however, before entering the ring, even if she is a short-haired dog. If she's long-coated, you should take all the paraphernalia necessary to spruce her up at the show.

Take along a bowl and a jug of water and a few treats for a reward when she's performed her best. It's a good idea to include her crate so you can look at booths or visit the cafeteria.

You may want a station wagon to haul home your trophies as well! But the most important things to take (besides Dixie) are patience and a sense of humor, so both you and your dog will have a good time.

What should I wear?

Most handlers pick clothing that is practical, yet attractive. Bright colors abound, often chosen to match or contrast with their dogs. A fire-engine red dress looks great with a Dalmatian, and a gray suit sets off the flame in an Irish Setter's coat.

Men usually wear suits or sport coats with slacks. Sometimes the choice is a sweater or sport shirt rather than a jacket, particularly in obedience, where the attire is often more casual. Women's fashions vary from dresses and suits to neat slacks or culottes. At the most formal shows, such as National Specialties or Westminster Kennel Club, some handlers don tuxedos. All of these outfits, including the tuxes, usually include a bait pocket and a good pair of running shoes as accessories. The dog's gait should be smooth, so most women don't wear impractical shoes that may cause them to trip. Choose outfits that draw attention to your dog, not you.

It's a good idea to pack a raincoat in the car and to dress in layers, so that you can add to or take off clothing as the weather changes.

My daughter wants to show our Gordon Setter. What are the regulations for children showing dogs?

Your daughter has the choice of 4-H, junior handling classes, obedience, or breed ring competition. The only requirement regarding obedience or conformation is that the handler be able to control the dog. In 4-H and junior showmanship competition, participants are judged solely on their ability as handlers, although a well-behaved, well-groomed dog is an asset.

AKC junior class divisions are Novice Junior, Novice Senior, Open Junior, and Open Senior. Novice Junior is for boys and girls ten to thirteen years of age who have not won a first place in a Novice class at a licensed show. Open Junior is for the same age group with a first-place win. The Senior classes hold the same requirements for ages thirteen to seventeen. (Occasionally, boys and girls compete separately.)

Dogs must be owned or co-owned by the junior handler or by the handler's father, mother, brother, sister, uncle, aunt, grandparent, or corresponding step- or half-relatives. The dog must be eligible for competition in AKC shows.

Judges may ask questions, such as "What color is disqualifying in your breed?" or "Where is your dog's stifle?" Therefore, the juniors should study the breed Standards and general conformation of dogs. Because the juniors are often highly skilled and proficient (sometimes more so than their adult counterparts), elusive tactics are sometimes used by judges to determine the handler's confidence and knowledge. For instance, a judge may move a leg into an incorrect position to see whether the junior will correct it. Another maneuver is to move behind the handler. A handler should never block the judge's view of her dog, so the junior should move to the other side.

She should keep her dog looking its best at all times but should not overhandle to the point of seeming fidgety or of making her dog nervous. She should keep one eye on the judge and one on the dog, not always easy!

Many juniors have been raised at dog shows, and the terminology and techniques are second nature to them, giving a challenge to new-comers. But competitors who are willing to take that challenge are able to learn about all dogs and especially their chosen breed from the kennel floor up. They have the opportunity to form special relationships with their dog and other juniors, as well as preparing themselves for the future.

That future may involve dogs: breeding, professional handling, judging, even veterinary work. But, at the least, junior showmanship forms the basis for confidence, responsibility, healthy competition, and good sportsmanship—fundamentals for any future life.

I've heard about Champions. What other titles can I put on Lance, and how do you win all of these?

Championships (CH) are the only titles awarded in conformation showing and are completed by obtaining fifteen points, as allotted by AKC according to how many dogs Lance defeats. These points must be awarded by a minimum of three judges and must include at least two majors (shows of three to five points). AKC annually assigns points to regions according to a complicated system of registrations and show entries.

Obedience, however, offers many possibilities. After three "legs" are obtained in Novice, the dog is given a Companion Dog (CD) title. Open brings a Companion Dog Excellent (CDX), Utility a UD or Utility

Dog, and Tracking a TD or TDX for advanced work. After all of that, you may continue competing toward an Obedience Trial Championship (OTCH), which may be obtained by winning firsts and seconds in Open B and Utility classes at trials. Lance must garner at least three first placements, at least one each in Open B and Utility, and amass one hundred points based on the number of dogs defeated.

UKC offers similar titles, which all precede the name. UKC Champions must have one hundred points won under at least three different judges and must have been named Best Male or Female in Show. The Grand Show Championship is given to a dog winning three Champion of Champion classes under three judges. Obedience titles are very similar to AKC's although exercise requirements are somewhat different.

In addition, parent clubs honor dogs with various other awards, such as the Register of Merit for the ability to produce Champions or titlewinners.

Someone told me I need a pro handler. What are the advantages?

Professional handlers have the benefits of experience, finesse, and knowledge on their side, but many amateurs have been able to achieve similar attributes with hard work. Others, however, are born klutzes and can't walk across the ring without tripping over their dogs. Because the main object of showing dogs is to have yours look good and to win, many owners who lack the skill, confidence, or physical ability hire a pro to do the job.

The pros try to make their dogs look as good as possible, maybe even better. It's their business to win. If they can't do that, they eat meatloaf instead of steak the rest of the week. They study the judges to learn which ones love good movement and take their supermoving Bloodhound or Saluki under those; their elegant Tibetan Terrier and Irish Setter are entered under the ones who appreciate a good coat.

Although handlers' services aren't cheap, using one may actually be more reasonable than attending the shows yourself if you calculate the expenses involved. Some owners chose to have and eat their cake, however, by hiring a handler and going to watch the excitement.

It's up to you which way you want to go. But another object of dog shows is to have fun, so if you prefer to get in the ring and do battle yourself, go for the gold!

A judge told me Thor needs roadwork. Why? How?

Thor may lack proper muscling for his breed and age. Roadworking strengthens backs, builds muscle, and increases stamina. Before the dog is one year of age, strenuous exercise can be harmful to immature bones, but after maturity, you can work him by foot, bicycle, car, or treadmill. Jogging or running with Thor helps you as well as your dog, but often a human cannot run fast enough or long enough to give the dog the workout he needs. Biking works well as long as you can keep your dog out of your way, or you'll take some nasty tumbles and you'll both wind up in traction instead of in the ribbons.

If you decide to roadwork Thor by car, make certain the dog is not frightened of the vehicle, drive slowly, and ask someone else to hold the leash and observe the dog so he doesn't slip or tire. Treadmills furnish the perfect solution to the lazy owner or one with several dogs who need work. They are expensive, however, and don't do *your* waistline a bit of good!

What is a benched show?

Dogs are placed on a platform display area supplied by the club and must stay in their place during specific show hours, unless being exercised or shown. These shows are big draws for spectators, because they can usually view a wide variety of dogs.

Exhibitors often enjoy them too, because they are a break in the normal routine: drive to the show, groom your dog, show your dog, go home. Sometimes they decorate their benches or arrange potluck lunches. Benched shows also offer an opportunity for breeders to show off their wares and to garner interest in their breed or an upcoming litter. Only seven benched shows are held in the United States at this time, although, at one time, they were the rule. They've decreased in popularity because they take a great deal of space (therefore money), as well as requiring the losers—not just the winners—to stay all day. Most losers prefer to slip quietly away.

Will hunting ruin a show dog?

The call of the wild is beckoning dog owners back to nature. Instinctive activities are being encouraged: herding, terrier trials, carting, lure coursing, sled dog racing, and hunting. Utilizing the dog's natural abilities gives the owner and dog immense satisfaction and usually augments rather than deters a dog's performance in the show ring. It is the best way to firm up spongy muscles. Hunting dogs may be hampered in growing a profuse coat, and either coat or instinct may have to be sacrificed until one career takes precedence.

Can I show Mimi without papers?

If you have an ILP number (see p. 37), you may enter Mimi in obedience trials. Even without an individual or single listing, you may enter her in fun matches and mixed-breed trials. Look up the *New England Obedience News* address under Helpful Addresses (p. 188) for more information on mixed-bred obedience competition and titles.

Every year there's a fun match in the park. Is that the same thing as a show?

Sanctioned matches as described previously offer classes for puppies, starting as young as two months of age. These are held as proving grounds for clubs that wish to be approved for point shows, for young or old dogs needing practice, and for young or old handlers needing practice and confidence! They also provide a source of income for the club and a social event for everyone.

"Fun" matches are not sanctioned by a kennel authority and are usually hosted by a group of dog lovers. Here you can find classes for Owner and Dog Look-Alike, Parade of Champions, Biggest/Smallest Dog, Best Trick, Hairiest, Baldest, Fastest, Oldest, Most Unusual Name, Best Groomed, and more. Obstacle courses and Best Pooch Smooch add to the festivities.

Matches are more relaxed and casual than shows but are just as much fun!

What does Tracking involve?

It involves following your nose, at least for the dog. Training begins with a tracking harness and fifty feet of light line, such as a nylon clothesline. Although a dog has probably been tracking all its life—from its first blind beeline for mother's milk to its trek to the food bowl or to a lost toy—classes teach the owner to help the dog follow a particular scent on command.

To earn a Tracking title on his dog, the owner must be sold on

the subject. It means rising at dawn to track while the dew is still on
the field, finding various terrains and large areas to lay trails, and hiking
over hill, dale, muck, and mud to do so.

Dogs must be certified to ascertain their readiness, although they
need pass only once to obtain their title. The track is 440 to 500 yards
long, laid by a stranger, and aged from thirty minutes to two hours.
The handler must follow at least 20 feet behind the dog and cannot
guide him in following the tracklayer's scent, except through limited
verbal encouragement. Legs of the track are straight, with right-angle
turns, and may be laid into or away from the wind.

The dog must work continuously, ground sniffing (rather than air
scenting) close to the track, and find the jackpot—the scented glove.
If you and your dog find this exciting, you can proceed to the TDX,
with a longer, more complicated, and more aged trail, for "xpert"
trackers.

15

No Bed of Roses

What would be considered animal abuse?

Abuse is the physical or mental pain inflicted on another living being, including beating, withholding medical care, and not providing water, food, or shelter. Neglect is also abusive, because it often becomes physically and/or mentally injurious.

Why would anybody abuse a dog?

People who are compassionate find it hard to believe the unspeakable cruelties living creatures, particularly defenseless beings, suffer at the hands of some others. But it does occur, many times every day. Much of this results from ignorance or neglect. When one is overwhelmed with pressures, poverty, or responsibility, pet care becomes low on the list of priorities. In these instances, either humane education or removal of the pet usually takes care of the situation. In other cases, the perpetrator is a bully or has a perverted quirk. This type of person should never own an animal.

If I see someone harming an animal, what can I do?

Do not endanger yourself if you feel interference will turn the perpetrator's wrath on you, but do report the incident to the proper authorities. Note the address, time, and other specifics for a full report, so the humane organization can conduct a thorough investigation. Teaching children to be gentle and caring to animals is a positive step toward making them compassionate adults. Set good examples for them to follow. Research shows that many prison inmates began by abusing animals and "worked their way up" to humans.

Where do I call?

The best person to talk to is the local animal control officer. Other good choices would be the American Society for Prevention of Cruelty to Animals (ASPCA) or the local police department. The ASPCA has lobbied for legislation to protect animals, and all municipalities have methods of enforcing these laws.

Why are so many (millions) healthy animals euthanized each year?

This is a throwaway world. We've become used to buying impulsively and disposing of our purchase when the newness wears off, when we find something else to take its place, or when it is no longer attractive or convenient. We use tissues instead of handkerchiefs. We trade in our cars every couple of years. We change jobs, houses, or mates when we find more appealing ones.

People tend to buy dogs on a whim, and too often their spur-of-the-moment purchases become throwaway pets. When the owners wake up to reality and find their caprice is a living being that needs to be fed and walked every single day—vacation, holiday, lousy weather, even when owners are sick—their enthusiasm wanes. Perhaps the dog doesn't housebreak as easily as hoped, or it has grown larger than expected. Or the family's moving and doesn't want to be bothered. Maybe their bitch became pregnant, or an old dog developed some problems they didn't want to deal with. Many of these people take the easy way out and turn in the throwaway pet at an animal shelter, which is preferable to unnecessary euthanizing or dumping it as a street orphan. At least the dog has a chance, not much more than the proverbial snowball, but a small chance. They don't think about the fear and confusion the animal suffers.

Most people mistakenly believe, however, that their white elephant will be another person's treasure. They honestly feel someone else will be happy to give a home to their wastebasket dog.

Shelters keep castoffs for varying lengths of time, depending on available space and the dog's adoptability. The pet most likely to be adopted is young and healthy. Attractive, trained, and well-behaved animals are more appealing to prospective owners. In fact, animal control officers state that the canine equivalent of a "blond, blue-eyed infant boy" is under three months, will stay small, and has long blond or white hair. Those that are not adopted are euthanized or, in the case of a no-kill facility, serve a life sentence in the shelter.

What can I do to help animals?

Dog lovers can work to reduce the aforementioned statistics by encouraging lawmakers to pass regulations protecting animals and giving higher penalties to abusers. Abuse is considered a misdemeanor, and the fine may be as low as fifty dollars, hardly a deterrent. They can also help to make certain their community has well-managed facilities to keep homeless animals. All shelters welcome volunteers and donations (food, coupons, towels, flea shampoo, bowls, as well as money). Just call and ask; they'll be happy to tell you what their particular needs are.

Most important, think of the amazing number of animals annually killed before you make a spur-of-the-moment purchase or before you breed your bitch. Neutering all pets would lower these numbers tremendously. The world doesn't need more dogs! Recent figures show that professional breeders of purebreds produce less than 10 percent of all canines in the United States. Disreputable puppy mills add an equal number, with strays contributing another 1 percent to the total. More than 79 percent of all puppies come from the pet owner, through accidental breedings or various not-good-enough reasons.[1]

---

[1] Janice Mullen-Stewart, "You, Your Dog and the Law," *Pure-Bred Dogs/American Kennel Gazette* (July 1987).

I made a mistake. A dog just doesn't fit into my life at this time. What should I do with him?

First, call the breeder you bought him from. Professional breeders are usually willing to take one of their pups back because they don't want him to become a statistic. Oftentimes they have a waiting list of prospective buyers so your dog can find a new home with a minimum of adjustment and shuffling.

If that is impossible, pass the word among friends, tell your vet, and advertise for a good home. Because your dog is housebroken, has had his shots, and perhaps has been trained and neutered, you'd think his value would be increased. The reverse is often true, however, because most people want a puppy. Adults are a dime a dozen, so be prepared to reduce your price—perhaps to zero.

You can take him to an animal control center, bearing in mind the low percentage of adoptions (30 percent out of the millions of dogs turned in). At least he'll be fed and cared for during his remaining time.

I just moved and my apartment landlord doesn't allow dogs. What can I do with Apollo?

Find a new apartment where dogs are welcome. If that's not feasible, you can try reasoning with your landlord. Offer to pay a damage deposit. You may be able to impress the apartment manager with Apollo's quiet behavior and marvelous personality. If you can, impress her with an obedience routine. Talk to other tenants and ask whether they'd be interested in signing a petition in favor of pets. The 1983 Federal Fair Housing Act gives tenants the right to keep their pets in federally assisted housing for the elderly or handicapped.

If you have no luck with these courses of action, try to find someone who will be willing to adopt Apollo and allow you visitation rights. Many people in this situation see no other recourse, however, than to find their dog another home and learn to read the fine print of a lease.

My favorite aunt is going to be entering a nursing home soon, and I know she will miss her pets. I'm going to take both Pokey and Gigi, but what else can I do to help her?

Nursing homes, among other institutions, have recently proved the value of pets in therapy and health maintenance. Some have a resident mascot, and you may be fortunate enough to find one of these homes. Others that do not have the staff or facilities to offer this advantage schedule routine get-togethers with local dog lovers and their animals. You may be able to arrange to have Pokey and Gigi visit your aunt or take her out for an afternoon to see them.

Amazing breakthroughs have occurred through these therapy animals. Sometimes it's easier for an Alzheimer's syndrome victim, autistic child, or mentally disturbed patient to talk to someone who listens but doesn't judge or offer advice, just cuddly warmth and kisses. Because of this discovery, more and more places are putting out the welcome mat for visitations from pets.

My trailer park has a rule: "No more than two dogs, and when those two die, they cannot be replaced." Isn't that sad?

It is sad, made all the more so by the fact that dog owners have brought this ruling upon themselves. If wishes could come true, everyone with a dog would stop its barking, clean up after it, and never allow it to run unconfined. Loose dogs dump garbage, frighten people, damage property, and sometimes bite, so the manager's rule is understandable. If the dog is large, the close quarters of a trailer park magnify poor behavior.

What's even more distressing is the fact that many residents of trailer parks are elderly and truly need the companionship of a pet.

You can try calling a meeting of all inhabitants, talking this over among yourselves, and approaching the manager with a proposition. If residents agree to set terms, police the area, and enforce rules, your manager just may agree. Maybe he's a dog lover himself.

How do I find out what ordinances in my district concern dogs?

Most libraries have copies of ordinances. You can also find the necessary information by calling the city attorney's or town clerk's office. The local humane officer may also be able to inform you of regulations.

Why should I pay good money for a dog tag?

Think of the tag as a positive step toward ensuring your dog's safety. If your pet is lost, you can be traced through the tag. Your pet doesn't carry a wallet with Social Security card, driver's license, and charge cards for identification. The tag on his collar proves he's vaccinated for rabies and serves as an ID that can bring him back to you. You're also helping dogs less fortunate than yours, because some of the fees help support humane organizations.

Jazmin has been sick for a long time. I can't stand the thought of her dying.

Ideally, each of our pets would leave us at a ripe old age and with no pain. We should have time to adjust ourselves to their death. But there's never enough time. No matter what the age of the dog, if we love her, it is always too soon. Nevertheless, it is good that life is this way, for as brutally painful as it is to lose pets, it would be worse by far for them to lose us, for we are their gods.

Counselors now know pet bereavement cannot be ignored or taken lightly. Professional journals are covering the subject in depth. The Veterinary Hospital of the University of Pennsylvania in Philadelphia has a full-time pet bereavement counselor. Look in Suggested Reading (pp. 191–92) for books on this subject.

I couldn't possibly make the decision to end Saber's life. What should I do?

Euthanasia is a unique situation open to pet owners. A compassionate resolution can be made to end pain or an inability to function. Perhaps in this way, animals have an advantage over us. But this verdict does place a burden of pain and guilt upon the person who chooses this option.

If you cannot make this decision, nature will finally make it for you. In the meantime, however, your beloved pet may suffer needlessly and look at you with eyes pleading for reprieve. Saber's veterinarian can aid you in making the final decision. Vets, like physicians, want to save lives, not end them, so their advice will not be given without good reason. They have the experience to help you decide when the time is right. Ultimately, it will still be you who has to make the choice: whether to answer Saber's plea or let his torment continue.

The following memorial written by a pet lover says it all:

Her soft, brown eyes reflected her love and she did everything we asked of her. She did it all until the end, when my heart wanted her to be young again, to start all over. This time she couldn't do what I wanted, so I did what she wanted. I let her go.

How do I know it's time to put an end to my pet's suffering?

Some animals are stoic and bear pain more easily than others. We can prolong their lives with veterinary help and TLC until pain or function loss becomes unbearable to us and undignified to them. A time comes when we must put aside our feelings and think about what is best for the dog. When living is more painful than dying, it's time.

I know what's got to be done, but I can't go with Camille on this final trip.

All her life, your dog has trusted you. Although this is a distressing crisis to face, do not desert her at a time when she needs you most. Sending Camille off with strangers, frightened, will only make the end more traumatic for her. Give her your love and support until the last moment. Reassure her your love is so great you are allowing her to go in peace. Repay your pet for years of devotion with your caress until the end.

Is euthanasia painful?

The only thing your dog will feel is the prick of the needle, similar to that of a shot. Some veterinarians tranquilize the dog first, so that he is drowsy during the lethal dose. Either way, the veterinarian administers an overdose of anesthetic that stops the heart. It is swift (fewer than thirty seconds) and humane.

I've had my old girl a long time. When Suzy goes, can I bury her?

Burial of pets at home is regulated by local laws. Urban areas often have restrictions. Talk to your vet to see whether he has or knows of a pet cemetery; these are becoming more common. Cremation is also an option.

What can I do for my neighbor, Jane, while she's in the hospital? She has two dogs she's worried about.

Concerned people thoughtfully take chicken broth, tuna noodle casseroles, and banana bread to friends and family but usually forget about the four-legged members of the household. Worrying about their pets' well-being can hamper a recovery. You would ease your friend's mind if you offered to care for her dogs during her illness and recuperation. Feed, exercise, brush, and caress them, and relate all their antics to their owner. Then see Jane smile!

What would happen to Lady and Toto if something happened to me?

Unless family members take the "orphans" into their homes and hearts, Lady and Toto will be picked up by an animal control officer and suffer the same fate as any dog taken to the pound.

Worse, if no one knows about your pets or Lady and Toto are not found during the upset of your death and the aftermath, they may suffer extreme discomfort or even starve before they are discovered.

What should I do to protect them?

Decide who can provide the best home for your pets and determine whether they would be willing to do so. Attach a codicil to your will, with a Statement of Intent to be used in the interim. The Statement can make your wishes known immediately without a long wait for probate. Give copies to friends, neighbors, family members, and your veterinarian, and place one in a safety deposit box.

You may want to provide a trust fund so that the financial care of your pets will not be a burden. Update your Statement as changes occur in your pet situation.

As a serious step in owner responsibility, a foster home should be considered as carefully as the first step taken to purchase a pet. You are the best person to judge the ideal situation for a beloved friend and to leave instructions. You alone know whether your dog likes children, loves outdoor exercise, is prone to bladder infections, or is allergic to chicken.

Your decision may even be that the best place for your pet is in his final resting place. This can be the case if your dog is elderly, debilitated, aggressive, or painfully shy, precluding a change of homes. In this situation, talk over the possibility with your veterinarian. Be certain of her understanding and agreement; note that in your Statement.

Include identification of your pets, preferably with a picture. All Labs may look alike to someone who doesn't know the difference between Blackie, Midnight, and Carbon. Be sure to give complete directions regarding food and medication.

If you should predecease your pets or become disabled and unable to care for them, it will be too late to provide for their well-being. Do it now.

16
Puppourri

I love dogs and would like to work with them—any suggestions?

Many careers are available to satisfy dog lovers, varying from long years of formal training to self-taught vocations and avocations. Whether working directly or indirectly with canines, it's your choice, depending on your particular interest, ambition, and capabilities. The most obvious choice is veterinarian, if you are prepared for many years of demanding education. Today doctors of veterinary medicine have a wide field in which to pick a specialty: surgery, reproduction, radiology, cardiology, neurology, ophthalmology, and internal medicine. Many vets are focusing their attention on special interests, for example, research, oncology, dentistry, geriatrics, dermatology, canine pediatrics, or behavior psychology. The two-year veterinary technician programs are attracting more and more interest among those who like to work with dogs.

If you love dog shows, you can become a professional breeder, handler, supply booth operator, or show photographer. Groomers, training class instructors, supply warehouse managers, writers on dog-related subjects, pet supply operators, dog magazine publishers, training school owners, and boarding kennel operators all aid the pet owner as well as the avid exhibitor.

In addition, trainers and handlers of special-purpose dogs—police, hunting, mine or drug detection, search and rescue work, or dogs for the blind, deaf, and handicapped—are in demand. If you're not looking for a career, but merely a part-time involvement, volunteer at a humane society, where dogs hunger for just such love as you have to give.

Do dogs see in color?

For many years, dogs were thought to be color-blind. Recently, however, microscopic studies of the retina have shown that it is possible they see tones.

Owners have also conducted their own "tests," telling their dogs to pick the yellow ball out of a pile of red and blue ones. Unless they are all new toys, however, it would be difficult to tell whether a dog chose the yellow ball or his favorite, good-smelling ball. Even if all were carefully descented and untouched by human hands, the correct selection could be just luck. Until one of us is reincarnated from a former life as a canine, we will never know.

How many human years equal a dog year?

An old wives' tale claimed seven human years equal each one of a dog's. Canines become physically mature and able to reproduce around one year of age; this is not equivalent to the maturity of a seven-year-old child. Therefore, a new chronology chart has been made for comparison:

Dog	Human
6 months	10 years
8 months	13 years
10 months	14 years
12 months	15 years
18 months	20 years
2 years	24 years
4 years	32 years
6 years	40 years

8 years	48 years
10 years	56 years
11 years	60 years
12 years	64 years
13 years	68 years
14 years	72 years
15 years	76 years
16 years	80 years
18 years	88 years
20 years	96 years
21 years	100 years

Why on earth would Jock want to eat his own (or another animal's) stool?

This habit is termed *coprophagia* and is particularly disgusting to owners. The culprit has bad breath and is susceptible to germs and parasites. This practice is totally incomprehensible to humans, but to dogs stools have an inexplicable attraction. Brood matrons clean up after their puppies, and sometimes this instinct continues long after the pup is bigger than they are. Other causes could be a poor-quality diet or undigested food in the stool, but some dogs just seem to be born "recyclers." The unemptied cat litter box and horse or cow pies in the pasture may also tempt him.

Clean up your yard often, keep your dog on lead when walking, empty the litter box frequently, and isolate it. Feed Jock plenty of high-quality dry food, with a small amount of canned meat. Several products can be added to Jock's diet to curb this aberration, but the best remedy is instant cleanup.

Why does Indy circle before he lies down?

Sometimes dogs show instincts that have been ingrained since cave-dog days, and we can only guess at the reasons. Probably this is related to nesting and making a comfy bed, or it may be a protective trait, with Indy checking out what is behind him so he won't be attacked as he sleeps. It is one of those unanswerable questions, but an endearing trait, like chasing tails.

Why does Jade scratch at the floor?

Back in the days of yore, when dogs were wild and had to make their own beds, rather than share yours, they scratched a stack of comfy leaves, straw, or dried grass together to make themselves a nice, cozy nest. Females, particularly brood matrons, are more prone to this habit than males. Nesting prior to labor and delivery is a common trait among expectant dams.

What makes Brock "sing" at some noises?

A dog's hearing is more acute than ours—that's why Brock can hear a dog whistle when we can't or hear your husband's truck when it's three blocks away. Therefore, some noises, particularly high-pitched sounds (like sirens), trigger his response. He just can't help joining in enthusiastically, as we do when we hear a barbershop quartet harmonizing an old, familiar tune.

Can dogs see in the dark?

Sight is one sense that is not keener in dogs than in humans. Although their peripheral vision is greater, canine depth perception is not astute; they perceive with both eyes about what we do with one. Most are nearsighted, and the bird they seem to "see" across the field is actually noted by scent or by a flash of movement.

If they manage to wend their way through a completely darkened room, it's due to their sense of scent and a memory of familiar objects in their usual places. When the room is dimly lit, however, dogs aren't as likely to stumble over a footstool. Their eyes have a reflecting layer that enables them to take advantage of existing light, whether a neon sign outdoors or a reflection from another room.

What is a quick way to muzzle a dog if necessary?

A leash serves well as a muzzle or, in lieu of that, nylons or a belt will suffice. Loop the leash around the muzzle twice, tight enough so that the dog will not be able to bite, then tie behind the ears.

I have a breed that is supposed to have erect ears. What should I do if Spock's don't stand up?

All dogs are born with floppy ears. Erect ears begin to lift by six to eight weeks and are usually firm by three months. Stubborn ones with heavy cartilage (called "ear leather") are often taped or braced to encourage them to stand. Taping instructions can be found in books or articles on your breed. Your veterinarian or breeder should also be able to assist you in pointing Spock's ears in the right direction. Few ears refuse to stand unless taping is begun too late; by the time teething is complete at six or seven months, ears are set for life.

I'd like to donate a dog for a dog guide. Whom do I contact?

Several training schools exist in the United States (see Helpful Addresses, pp. 188–89). Native Philadelphian Dorothy Harrison Eustis raised working German Shepherds at Fortunate Fields, a chalet in Switzerland. She donated a trained dog named Kiss (soon renamed Buddy) to Morris Frank, who became the first blind person aided by a dog guide in the United States. In 1929, after his success, Frank, along with Eustis and trainer Jack Humphrey, established Seeing Eye, Inc., the first of many schools that train dog guides, match them with applicants, and enable the sightless to live with more independence.

These canine assistants are trained for "intelligent disobedience," which means that if someone directs them "Forward" into the path of a car, they refuse to obey. And if a master wants to walk straight ahead into a low-hanging tree branch or ditch, the guide takes a detour or blocks his path. This requires a highly intelligent dog who is capable of thinking rather than obeying implicitly.

What are the requirements?

First of all, the dog must be purebred, in good health, and have x-rayed normal hips. They prefer receiving the animal when it is about one year old, ready to begin training immediately. Most dog guides are spayed females. Occasionally, neutered males are used, but they tend to be too large for the average person to hold comfortably on harness. In addition, the leg-hiking habit is hard to break. German Shepherds are the most frequently chosen, with a good number of Golden and Labrador Retrievers and a sprinkling of other breeds.

My mother is deaf and has read about hearing dogs. Please tell me about them.

Organizations that train dogs to assist the hearing-impaired (see Helpful Addresses, pp. 188–89) perform two good deeds. A canine can be taught to respond to doorbells, oven-timers, telephone rings—anything its master needs. A hearing dog can help a mother who can't hear her baby crying, wake a man when his alarm rings, or save a family if the smoke alarm sounds. And these dogs are chosen from animal shelters, so trainers not only provide a service for the deaf but save a life.

After the dog is accomplished in the basics, the trainer takes him to the proposed home. In this environment, the dog is taught the intricacies of his specialized job, and the prospective owner learns how to respond and becomes acquainted with her new "ears." These organizations are run through donations and funding. Animals who aid the deaf are given the same rights as dog guides and are allowed to accompany their owners on public transportation, into stores, and in restaurants.

Where does the military service get dogs for defense purposes?

More than two thousand dogs currently are employed by the Department of Defense. Some were born "army brats"; others were recruited from civilian life. These dogs must be sturdy, one to three years old, a minimum of sixty pounds and twenty-three inches, and x-rayed free of hip dysplasia. The rookies, which must be German Shepherd or Belgian Malinois, are tested for bravery in the face of gunshots and agitation. They must be sound in temperament and able to follow commands. Even after testing and training, about 25 percent don't make the grade mainly because they won't bite or attack, and they are given back their "civvies."

I have a handicapped daughter who wants to be out on her own. Where can we go for help?

Think of a constant companion who'll push the elevator button for your daughter, one who will pick up the coin she dropped, hand her the phone, or open doors. That's a good friend, particularly if she can't do these things for herself. Dogs don't judge. They're your friends whether you can walk or not. Support Dogs for the Handicapped and Canine Companions for Independence (see Helpful Addresses, pp. 188–89) are coached in sundry activities to assist the handicapped.

Many of the dogs are chosen from animal shelters, another satisfying factor. Because of the strength needed to lift a helpless person's weight, most are large: German Shepherds, Golden and Labrador Retrievers, Standard Poodles, Doberman Pinschers, and the Belgian shepherd breeds. They're taught to stand still, bearing the weight of their owners who are pulling themselves to their feet. They pull wheelchairs up ramps and hills. At all times, they're braced to break a fall. These dogs aid people who thought they could never live alone to be independent.

Toma snores. What do I do?

Brachycephalic dogs and others with elongated soft palates often "saw wood." Check with Toma's doctor to see if there's a medical cause. If not, you can move his sleeping quarters, or yours, or buy a pair of earplugs.

When Morgan is sleeping, she makes strange whimpering noises. What causes this?

She's chasing bunnies! Or perhaps she's climbing the Andes, swimming the English Channel, or leading the famed Iditarod, the sled dog race. Who knows whether dogs dream? But if they do, let's hope they're all sweet dreams.

I've heard rawhide bones can be dangerous. Why?

Dogs who tear rawhide asunder and swallow large pieces may have trouble digesting the chunks. In fact, blockage of the intestine can occur, sometimes necessitating surgery. Watch your pet as he plays with his toys. If he has the appetite and table manners of a starving lion, you'd better choose a sturdier toy that he can't destroy and swallow.

Do people and dogs take after one another?

Maybe, in the way long-married mates do, not so much in looks but in temperament and mannerisms. Likes attract, and an outdoorsman is likely to choose an athletic dog, whereas a smart dresser will probably have a natty pet. A couch potato would prefer a canine counterpart snoozing next to him, rather than one tugging on his sleeve for a walk six times a day.

Why are dogs called man's best friend?

More than any other animal, dogs follow humans by choice, from the tagalong puppy to the adoring oldster. From time immemorial, they have served people and been our companions. They've been on earth for millions of years and will, we hope, be here forever more. But they're not only man's best friend—they're woman's best friend too.

APPENDICES

Plants Poisonous to Dogs

Following is a list of plants that can be poisonous to dogs, as explained in Chapter 9, page 88:

Common House Plants	Garden Flowers	Ornamental Plants
Caladium	Autumn crocus	Daphne
Castor bean	Bleeding heart	English ivy
Dieffenbachia	Foxglove	Gold chain
Dumb cane	Larkspur	Lantana
Elephant's ear	Lily of the valley	Mountain laurel
Philodendron	Monkshood	Yellow jessamine
Jerusalem cherry	Narcissus	Wisteria
Rosary pea	Daffodil	
Poinsettia	Jonquil	
Christmas rose		
Mistletoe		

Vegetables and Leaves	Trees and Shrubs (Leaves, Berries, Bark)	Field and Woods Plants
Tomato	Apricot	Buttercup
Potato	Avocado	Coneflower
Rhubarb	Azalea	Black-eyed Susan
	Black locust	Goldenglow
	Boxwood	Hemlock
	Horse chestnut	Jack-in-the-pulpit
	Chinaberry	Jimsonweed
	Wild black cherry	Mushrooms
	Holly	Nightshade
	Oak	American bitter-
	Oleander	sweet
	Privet	Deadly nightshade
	Rhododendron	Pokeweed
	Yew	White snakeroot
		Nettle
		Foxtail
		Sandbur

Glossary

AFCH (AFC) Amateur Field Champion

BIS Best in Show wins

CC Challenge Certificate, awarded toward Championships by the Kennel Club in England

CD (U-CD) Companion Dog

CDX (U-CDX) Companion Dog Excellent

CERF# Examined and found free of hereditary eye diseases by an ophthalmologist and then registered with the Canine Eye Registration Foundation, Inc.

CH Champion

FCH (FC) Field Champion

GCH UKC's award to Grand Champion

GV, GVX Grand Victor or Grand Victrix awarded by a Parent Club to the Best of Breed at the National Specialty

HCH Herding Champion; HC shows Herding Certificate for instinct test

HIT High in Trial (highest scoring dog in obedience)

Intl. CH International Champion: dog who wins a qualifying certificate, CACIB, in three International Dog Shows in three different countries, other than the United States, specified by rules of the FCI (Federation Cynologique Internationale)

JH Junior Hunter

MH Master Hunter

Nite CH Nite Champion (Coonhounds)

OFA# Sometimes noted by letters and a number, such as BC144, meaning Bearded Collie number 144, certified for having no signs of hip dysplasia, issued by the Orthopedic Foundation for Animals

OTCH Obedience Trial Champion

ROM Register of Merit, usually an award given by the Parent Club recognizing producing ability

SchH Schutzhund, a title of obedience, tracking, and protection tests

Sel Select at National Specialties

SH Senior Hunter

TD Tracking Dog

TDX Tracking Dog Excellent

TT Temperament tested

UD (U-UD) Utility Dog

Others, individual to the breed, may be given on a pedigree.

Helpful Addresses

KENNEL CLUBS
American Kennel Club, 51 Madison Avenue, New York, NY 10010
Canadian Kennel Club, 2150 Bloor Street W., Toronto, Ontario, M6S 4V7
United Kennel Club, 100 East Kilgore Road, Kalamazoo, MI 49001-5598

MAGAZINES/PERIODICALS
Bloodlines (UKC official magazine), 100 East Kilgore Road, Kalamazoo, MI 49001-5596
Canine Chronicle, P.O. Box 115, Montpelier, IN 47359
Dog Fancy, P.O. Box 53264, Boulder, CO 80322-3264
Dogs in Canada (CKC official magazine), 43 Railside Road, Don Mills, Ontario M3A 3L9
Dogs USA, Fancy Publications, Inc., P.O. Box 6040, Mission Viejo, CA 92690
Dog World, 29 North Wacker, Chicago, IL 60606
Front and Finish, P.O. Box 333, Galesburg, IL 61402
Kennel Review, 11331 Ventura Boulevard, Suite 301, Studio City, CA 91604

New England Obedience News (mixed-breed obedience titles), P.O. Box 105, Chicopee, MA 01021

Off-Lead, P.O. Box 307, Graves Road, Westmoreland, NY 13490

Pure-Bred Dogs/American Kennel Gazette (AKC official magazine), 51 Madison Avenue, New York, NY 10010

PRODUCTS

The Canine Consultant (videotapes on selecting and raising your dog), by Bardi McLennan, Bardwyn Productions, Inc., 25 Van Zant Street, East Norwalk, CT 06855

Creative Innovations International (vehicle restraint), 7900 Limonite Avenue, Suite g-123, Riverside, CA 92509

Custom Care Pet Supply, Inc. (pet car seat), 8124 Holy Cross Place, Los Angeles, CA 90045

Puppy Love (safety belt), P.O. Box 18021, West Palm Beach, FL 33416-8021

Saf-T Truck Harness, Custom Care Pet Supply, Inc., 8124 Holy Cross Place, Los Angeles, CA 90045

Sop-Up, Fin-Nel Corporation, 1300 Waynetown Road, Crawfordsville, IN 47933

SERVICES

American Rescue Dog Association, Goosepond Mountain State Park, P.O. Box 151, Chester, NY 10918

American Society for the Prevention of Cruelty to Animals, 441 East 92 Street, New York, NY 10028

Canine Companions for Independence, P.O. Box 446, Santa Rosa, CA 95402

Canine Eye Registration Foundation, Inc., P.O. Box 15095, San Francisco, CA 94115

Citizens Against Housing Discrimination for Pet Owners, Inc., P.O. Box 9901, Glendale, CA 91206

Department of Defense Dog Training Center, Headquarters San Antonio Air Logistics Center (AFLC), Lackland Air Force Base, San Antonio, TX 78236

Dogs for the Deaf, 13260 Highway 238, Jacksonville, OR 97530

Guide Dog Foundation for the Blind, 371 East Jericho Turnpike, Smithtown, NY 11787

Guide Dog Users, c/o 12 Riverside Street, Apt. 1-2, Watertown, MA 02172

Guide Dogs for the Blind, P.O. 1200, San Rafael, CA 94915

Guiding Eyes for the Blind, Yorktown Heights, NY 10598

Hearing Dog, Inc., 5901 East 89th, Henderson, CO 80640

Humane Society of the United States, 2100 L Street, NW, Washington, DC 20037

Leader Dogs for the Blind, 1039 South Rochester Road, Rochester, MI 48063-4887

National Dog Registry, Box 116, Woodstock, NY 12498

North American Hunting Retriever Association, Inc., P.O. Box 6, Garrisonville, VA 22463

Orthopedic Foundation for Animals, University of Missouri, Columbia, Columbia, MO 65201

Seeing-Eye Foundation, Morristown, NJ 07960

Support Dogs for the Handicapped, P.O. Box 28457, Columbus, OH 43228-0457

AKC LICENSED SUPERINTENDENTS

Antypas, William G., Jr., P.O. Box 7131, Pasadena, CA 91109

Bradshaw, Jack, P.O. Box 7303, Los Angeles, CA 90022

Brown, Norman E., P.O. Box 2566, Spokane, WA 99220

Crowe, Thomas J., P.O. Box 22107, Greensboro, NC 27420

Jones, Roy J. (Sleeper), P.O. Box 307, Garrett, IN 46738

Mathews, Ace H., P.O. Box 06150, Portland, OR 97206

Onofrio, Jack, P.O. Box 25764, Oklahoma City, OK 73125

Rau, James A., Jr., P.O. Box 6898, Reading, PA 19610

Roberts, B. Jeannie, P.O. Box 4658, Federal Way, WA 98063

Sweet, Mrs. Dorothy G., 2321 Blanco Road, San Antonio, TX 78212

CKC SUPERINTENDENTS

Ace Mathews Dog Shows, P.O. Box 06150, Portland, OR 97206

AL-Sec Associates, P.O. Box 8704, Station F, Calgary, Alta. T2J 5S4

C & A Show Services, Vin Vista Drive, Rural Route 3, Ingleside, Ont. K0C 1M0

Canadian Dog Show Services, P.O. Box 226, Station "J," Toronto, Ont. M4J 4Y1

Canine Show Services, Rural Route 2, Maple Avenue West, Brantford, Ont. N3T 5L5

Ho-Har Show Services, W. A. Hobbs, 341 Westwood Drive, Kitchener, Ont. N2M 3L3

Kam-Sec Associates, P.O. Box 1022, Station Main, Kamloops, BC V2C 6H1

Mike Williams Dog Shows, Box 718, Vernon, BC V1T 6M6

Pro-Cats, 1080 Brock Road, Unit 3, Pickering, Ont. L1W 3H3

Show & Trial Productions, Rural Route 1, Schomberg, Ont. L0G 1T0

Wes-Sec, 225 1 Wye Road, Sherwood Park, Alta. T8C 1H9

Suggested Reading

American Kennel Club. *The Complete Dog Book*. rev. ed. New York: Doubleday, 1986.

Anderson, Moira. *Coping with Sorrow on the Loss of Your Pet*. Los Angeles: Peregrine Press, 1987.

Bauman, Dianne. *Beyond Basic Dog Training*. New York: Howell Book House, 1986.

Benjamin, Carol Lea. *Dog Problems*. New York: Doubleday, 1981.

———. *Dog Training for Kids*. New York: Howell Book House, 1976.

———. *Mother Knows Best*. New York: Howell Book House, 1985.

Caras, Roger. *The Roger Caras Pet Book*. New York: Holt, Rinehart and Winston, 1976.

———. *Roger Caras' Treasury of Great Dog Stories*. New York: E. P. Dutton, 1987.

Carlson, Delbert G., D.V.M., and James M. Giffin, M.D. *Dog Owner's Home Veterinary Handbook*. New York: Howell Book House, 1981.

Clark, Ross, D.V.M., and Joan Stainer. *Medical and Genetic Aspects of Purebred Dogs*. Edwardsville, Kans.: Veterinary Medicine Publishing Co., 1983.

Curtis, Patricia. *Urban Dog: How to Understand, Enjoy and Care for a Dog in the City*. New York: Bantam Books, 1986.

Elliot, Rachel P. *The New Dogsteps*. rev. ed. New York: Howell Book House, 1983.

Evans, Job Michael. *Housetraining Your Dog*. New York: Howell Book House, 1987.

Gallop, Davia. *Running with Man's Best Friend*. Loveland, Colo.: Alpine, 1986.

Haggerty, Capt. Arthur J., and Carol Lea Benjamin. *Dog Tricks*. New York: Howell Book House, 1985.

Hancock, Judith M. *Friendship: You and Your Dog*. New York: E. P. Dutton, 1986.

Kirk, Robert W., D.V.M. *First Aid for Pets*. rev. ed. New York: E. P. Dutton, 1985.

Lanting, Fred. *Canine Hip Dysplasia*. Loveland, Colo.: Alpine, 1981.

The Monks of New Skete. *How to Be Your Dog's Best Friend*. Boston: Little, Brown, 1978.

Quackenbush, Jamie, M.S.W., and Denise Graveline. *When Your Pet Dies*. New York: Simon & Schuster, 1985.

Quinn, Tom. *The Working Retrievers*. New York: E. P. Dutton, 1983.

Siegal, Mordecai. *The Good Dog Book*. New York: The Macmillan Company, 1978.

Strickland, Winifred. *Expert Obedience Training for Dogs*. 2nd rev. ed. New York: The Macmillan Company, 1976.

Walkowicz, Chris, and Bonnie Wilcox, D.V.M. *Successful Dog Breeding: The Complete Handbook of Canine Midwifery*. New York: Arco/Prentice-Hall, 1985.

Wilcox, Bonnie, D.V.M., and Chris Walkowicz. *The Atlas of Dog Breeds: Dogs for All Reasons*. Neptune, N.J.: TFH Publications, 1988.

Wolters, Richard A. *Family Dog*. rev. ed. New York: E. P. Dutton, 1975.

———. *Game Dog*. New York: E. P. Dutton, 1983.

———. *Gun Dog*. New York: E. P. Dutton, 1961.

———. *Home Dog*. New York: E. P. Dutton, 1984.

———. *Kid's Dog*. new ed. New York: E. P. Dutton, 1984.

———. *Water Dog*. New York: E. P. Dutton, 1964.

Index